Orange County Housecleaners

Orange County Housecleaners

Frank Cancian

with

Julieta Noemi (Mimi) Lopez

Esperanza Mejia

Leidi Mejia

Tina Parker

Sharon Risley

Victoria Rua

Sara Velazquez

University of New Mexico Press
Albuquerque

10 09 08 07 06   1 2 3 4 5

Library of Congress Cataloging-in-Publication Data

Cancian, Frank.
  Orange County housecleaners / Frank Cancian ; with Julieta Noemi
(Mimi) Lopez ... [et al.].
        p. cm.
   ISBN-13: 978-0-8263-3687-3 (pbk. : alk. paper)
   ISBN-10: 0-8263-3687-6 (pbk. : alk. paper)
1. Women cleaning personnel—California—Orange County—Biography.
2. Women immigrants—California—Orange County—Social conditions.
3. Hispanic American women—California—Orange County—Biography.
I. Lopez, Julieta Noemi. II. Title.
    HD6073.C442C36 2006
    331.4'816485092368079496—dc22
                         2005025890

Photos followed by a date in parentheses are from the woman's
    family collection. The other photos were taken by
    Frank Cancian between spring 2000 and spring 2002.

Book design and type composition by Kathleen Sparkes
    This book was typeset using Utopia 10/15
    Display type is Futura Light

This book was printed in China
    by Everbest Printing Company, Ltd.

Contents

Victoria Rua 51

Victoria Rua lost touch with her children in Mexico in the 1970s when her husband was deported from the United States. He doubted her fidelity and cut off communication for ten years. They were reconciled almost twenty years ago. Recently she came to the United States to renew her papers and stayed to work, while he lives in Mexico on their small farm.

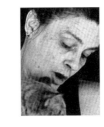

Sharon Risley 67

Sharon Risley earned a Bachelor of Fine Arts degree in 1990—twenty-six years after a teenage pregnancy destroyed her plans to go from high school to art school. Her steady work as a housecleaner began in the late 1980s, after her marriage broke up.

Esperanza Mejia 83

Esperanza Mejia has two reasons for not using her training as a medical assistant: because she was shocked by the way doctors treated her mother, who was visiting from Guatemala, and because housecleaning pays more and constrains her less in her role as a mother.

Julieta Noemi (Mimi) Lopez 99

Mimi Lopez was alone on Thanksgiving Day, 1985, when her twin daughters were born in the Miami house where she worked as a nanny/housekeeper. Two years ago, before the birth of her fourth child, she stopped cleaning houses—at least for the time being.

Preface

In this book seven women tell their life stories. I asked each one of them to begin with her childhood and to talk about whatever she thought was important in her life—and I recorded what she said.

The table of contents introduced you to their faces and to a few details from their stories. Each chapter will present one woman's story in her own words, along with my photographs of her, her family, and her activities. Most chapters also include photos from the woman's collection of family pictures. I believe that the combination of words and pictures provides a rich view of the person that neither pictures nor words could have done alone.

All the women work or recently worked as housecleaners. A short essay about their work world and its effects on their personal and family worlds follows this preface. It explains why housecleaners are usually seen as the elite of domestic workers. And it describes the difficult family situations often faced by Latin American immigrant women, who, in recent decades, have become the majority of domestic workers in Southern California.

The book grew out of a small project on five housecleaners I did in spring 2000. The people I met doing that project were so engaging that, a year later, I sought their help again and began putting this book together. I hope the words and pictures that follow will help you to enter their worlds and to understand them as they do.

For the most part, stories were recorded and photos were taken in summer and fall of 2001. When the present tense is used in the text, it refers to that period.

Frank Cancian
February 2005

Introduction

Domestic Workers in Southern California

I hope you will join me in approaching these stories and pictures in two ways—first, in a personal way, as you would approach any person talking about what is most important in her life, and second, as a social observer who looks at how a person's life relates to the social situation in which it takes place.

The personal approach uses what you bring with you—your own experience, your personal reaction to the story. I find that it also helps to talk with others about what I see. The more I do that, and the more I listen to them talk about what they see, the more I am able to see. I hope you will share your reactions to these stories and pictures with other people.

The social observer approach is based on background about the situation. For this book that means information about the jobs the women do, about the places they do them, and, for five of the women, about immigrants in Southern California. Fortunately, Pierrette Hondagneu-Sotelo has written an excellent book about immigrant Latina domestic workers in Los Angeles.* It throws light on the lives of domestic workers of all ethnicities.

Each of the next three sections summarizes points from her book and connects them to the lives of the seven women in this book. Since all the women who tell their stories here live and work just south of Los Angeles in Orange County, I've included a fourth section for readers who do not know Southern California. It provides a few details about Orange County's location, population, and recent history.

Housecleaners are different from nanny/housekeepers.

The lives of housecleaners are very different from those of most nanny/housekeepers. Housecleaners, the women in this book, usually work for many different employers. They clean one or more houses per day, and some of them rarely see

---

Pierrette Hondagneu-Sotelo, Doméstica: Immigrant Workers Cleaning and Caring in the Shadows of Affluence (University of California Press, 2001). If you want to learn more about the situation of domestic workers in Southern California, start with this book and the sources in its bibliography.

their employers. A nanny/housekeeper (both those who live in and those who live out) typically works full-time for a single family and does child care as well as housecleaning.

None of the women in this book live in a client's home. Six of the seven have several clients each week—often with a mix of every-week and every-other-week jobs and a mix of full-day and part-day jobs. For example, Victoria Rua cleans four houses every week and four others every other week. Her eight clients give her a six-day schedule of daylong jobs each week. Leidi Mejia's schedule includes one client that she works for one full day and one part day every week. Tina Parker, the only one of the seven who has a regular paid assistant, cleans more than twenty houses per week. Esperanza Mejia now works a five-day week for one of the many clients she had a few years ago and each Saturday cleans one of two other houses.

These diverse arrangements permit housecleaners like those in this book to control their schedules—and such arrangements lead some housecleaners to set themselves very demanding schedules. Because they have many employers, housecleaners are free to drop troublesome ones without great changes in their income or social relations. By contrast, nanny/housekeepers, especially those who live in, are more dependent on their employers. They often have personal ties to family members, especially the children.

Housecleaners usually earn more than nanny/housekeepers, and they often are paid by the job rather than by the hour or day. Nanny/housekeepers are usually paid by the week or the month.

Many women have done both jobs, usually at different times in their lives. Newly arrived immigrants, for example, often work as live-in nanny/housekeepers for a year or more while learning U.S. culture and ways of working—then move on to housecleaning. Four of the five Latina immigrants in this book followed this pattern—while the two native Anglos started doing domestic work as housecleaners.

The women in this book are among the most independent people who work as housecleaners. Many others work for agencies or companies that assign them to houses depending on the day's mix of customers and workers. Others live in one of the houses they clean and regularly spend some days each week cleaning other houses. Most housecleaners are women, some are men, and some couples work together.

Finally, housecleaners are often constrained by the demands of getting from home to jobs and from job to job in a reliable way. Victoria Rua and Sara Velazquez usually use the public bus system, as did Mimi Lopez when she worked. Esperanza Mejia, Leidi Mejia, Tina Parker, and Sharon Risley use their own vehicles. Before they got their own cars, Esperanza and Leidi also struggled with the bus system. As Leidi's story of her transition from public buses to her own car shows, transportation is important in many ways to life in Southern California.

Many domestic workers are mothers. This presents a special problem for immigrants who work as live-in nanny/housekeepers.

Very few employers want live-in nanny/housekeepers to have their own children with them, so immigrant mothers seeking domestic work typically leave their children with relatives in their native countries. They care for the children of their employers and live far from their own children in order to earn money to support them and finance plans for their futures.

Mimi Lopez, Esperanza Mejia, and Leidi Mejia came to the United States from Guatemala; Victoria Rua and Sara Velazquez came from Mexico. Sara, the most recent arrival among them, has been here for thirteen years. At one time or another each of them left one child or more with relatives in her home country while she worked to establish herself in the United States. Nine of the ten children they left are now living in the United States. Only Victoria Rua's daughter, who married in Mexico, has not come. Tina Parker and Sharon Risley were born and raised in Orange County.

Each of the immigrant women struggled to be a mother and an economic provider at the same time. Of course their situations differed. But in their stories you will see that separations from their families, especially their children, are followed, sometimes years later, by family conflicts—often by strains between mothers and children.

Domestic work is a growing occupation, and Latinas are a growing proportion of the workers.

More women in the United States have entered the workforce in the last three decades. As a result, more households wanted help with child care and housework. And more immigrants have been drawn to the job opportunities, especially when work and stability are in short supply in their home country.

Today the vast majority of women private household employees in the Los Angeles County and the Orange County metropolitan areas are Latinas. But that was not always so. In the Los Angeles area Latinas were 86 percent of female household employees in 2000. They were 23 percent in 1970. In the Orange County area, where they also were 86 percent in 2000, they were only 14 percent in 1970.*

It is hard to know exactly how this pattern shown in census data for household employees in general translates into numbers for housecleaners. My guess is that the proportion of Latina housecleaners is about the same. If that is so, to be representative of today's Southern California, this book would have to include six Latinas and only one non-Latina.

*These figures are based on Philip Cohen's analysis of data from Steven Ruggles and Matthew Sobek et al., "Integrated Public Use Microdata Series: Version 3.0" (Minneapolis: Historical Census Projects, University of Minnesota, 2003). Workers are included if they were employed in the previous year in one of these three occupations: private household workers (not otherwise classified), housekeepers (private household), or laundresses (private household).

Orange County for people who don't know it.

Orange County is on the Pacific coast in Southern California. It is between Los Angeles County to its north and San Diego County on its south; San Diego County borders Mexico. Los Angeles County has roughly ten million people. Orange and San Diego counties have about three million each. Together these three counties have 45 percent of the state's people. Riverside County, which also figures in one of the life stories in this book, stretches from the eastern border of Orange County to the Arizona border.

Los Angeles and San Diego counties orient to the very large cities whose names they share. Orange County has two smaller cities, each with about 350,000 people. Santa Ana is the county seat and a destination for many immigrants, especially those from Mexico and Central America. Seventy percent of its people speak Spanish at home. Anaheim is known as the home of Disneyland and, more recently, of baseball's World Champion Angels. Both cities are inland, miles from the coast and nearer the agricultural areas that were once the core of the county's economy.

As Orange County's population grew rapidly (from 216,000 in 1950 to almost three million in 2000), thousands of acres of orange groves and other agricultural land became residential, industrial, and commercial sites. These days the county is better known as a tourism center and for its high-tech manufacturing and research.

As you might guess, richer people tend to live closer to the coast (in the "Beach Cities"), and poorer people tend to live inland. The lives of domestic workers and other service workers follow this pattern. On the whole they live inland and work closer to the coast. Esperanza Mejia, Leidi Mejia, Mimi Lopez, and Sara Velazquez live in gated apartment complexes in inland cities adjacent to Santa Ana. Tina Parker lives in a rented house inland in the northwestern part of the county. Victoria Rua lived with a relative nearer the coast, then moved to a rented room in Santa Ana. These six women do most of their work in Newport Beach, Irvine, and other prosperous suburban cities. Sharon Risley has her own house and clients in Laguna Beach, a smaller city known as an art colony and destination for vacationers.

The contrasts in income and ethnicity between coast and inland areas are at their starkest when one compares Newport Beach and Santa Ana. Per capita income in Newport Beach is more than five times that in Santa Ana ($63,000 vs. $12,000 per year). English is the only language spoken in 87 percent of Newport Beach homes, while the comparable figure for Santa Ana is 20 percent.* Most other comparisons of cities within the county are not as sharp.

The stories and photographs that follow document the lives of seven individuals. I hope this background on domestic workers, recent immigration, and Southern California will help you place them in the context in which they live those lives.

*Figures from the 2000 census are rounded to the nearest thousand dollars/percent.

Sara Velazquez was born in Mexico. She came to the United States alone about thirteen years ago, leaving her husband, daughter, and three sons in Mexico. She and her husband now live in an apartment with their daughter and son-in-law and their two children. Their three sons and their families also live and work in Southern California.

Sara Velazquez

My name is Sara Mason Meneses [in the United States, Sara uses her husband's surname, Velazquez]. I'm Mexican. I come from a very humble family. My mother's name was Efijenia Meneses. She died. My father's name is Andres Mason. He's ninety-two. We were ten children: six brothers and four sisters. Like I said already, my family was very poor. But at the same time we were very happy, because being poor doesn't mean that you are not happy. I never thought that things happened to us because my parents were poor. I had a happy life.

I grew, went to school, and made friends. But my thinking was not as advanced as it is now. I was ignorant and not very good at things. My mother helped my father, and I helped her with her work, selling things in the market and baking things for sale. Her parents did not put her in school. She didn't know how to read. Only my father studied. He was a farmer. He seeded a lot of corn, and beans, and squash. This is what our mother gave us to eat. We ate meat once a week, if there was some.

I remember being very happy at Christmastime.

The Three Kings were coming again. What would they bring? I would go to bed early, because they said that if you didn't sleep, the Three Kings would not leave a gift. I got a doll—made out of cardboard. But I saw that Eva, my little girlfriend next door, got a doll that came in a box and had curls. One day I asked my mother why the Three Kings didn't bring me a doll like Eva's. And she said, "I'll tell you. That is the doll that richer people get. The poorer one comes here."

My two oldest sisters married young. I was the only one to marry at twenty-three. I think that's why I helped my mother so much. I studied until I got into secondary school, and then I decided I didn't want to continue, and I stopped. I got a job in the cafeteria at a teachers' college. I was very happy there because it was my adolescence—and that is the time girls get boyfriends. That time and my childhood were the happiest times of my life. That's what I tell my daughter. I'd like to go back to my childhood and the time when I had a boyfriend. But life goes on. It moves ahead, and here I am in the United States.

Sara with her father (between his daughters), sister, and six brothers.
Two sisters had passed away (1994).

To the United States

My husband used to say, "I'm going to go to the United States." I would hear it and say, "He's crazy about going there, but not me. Why would I go? I'm doing fine here." But you never know what will happen.

We've been together for thirty-five years, and I'll tell you something that happened when we had been married for fifteen years. My children were growing, and I could see that we lacked many things for them. I thought, Little by little, we'll get ahead. But then I had a problem I couldn't solve. My husband talked about going to the United States, but I was the one that did it—because of a problem [with her husband], and for the money. My youngest child was nine when I decided to do it.

I saw a friend who was already working here. She was visiting in December. She asked me if I was still living with Juan (my husband is named Juan), and I said, "Yes." And she said, "Let's go to the United States." And I said, "You're crazy. I'm not going." When I saw her a week later in the market, she said, "Sara, won't you come with me?" And I said no again. As the saying goes, the third time did it. She asked again, and I said, "I'll see what Juan says."

I told Juan, and he said, "If you want to go, go!" "Fine," I said. That's how I got his permission, and I didn't think much about it. Now I ask myself, "Why did he let me come like that? Could it be that he didn't love me?"

It was 1988. My friend told me, "I'm going on January fifteenth. You're coming with me?" And I said, "Yes, I'm going to go." But in my heart it was yes and no. "How am I going to leave my children?" The day arrived, and I came—the fifteenth of January, 1988.

We went for Laredo, Texas. We got off the bus in Laredo, Tamaulipas, and I said to myself, "What am I doing here?" I thought of my children, but I didn't think of my husband. I cried, and my friend told me to keep going, that soon we'd be where I could talk to them on the phone.

We stayed with a friend of hers for three days; then we crossed. They told us to wear shorts and to bring dry clothes in a bag. We got on a big tire tube, and we crossed with water coming up around my, pardon me, bottom and her sitting on top of me. How barbarous! But that's how we went. The water was really cold! We arrived, they told us to change to dry clothes, and soon there we were walking around the city of Laredo. I was sad thinking of my children. One minute I cried. The next minute I was happy.

I was there for eight months—working as a babysitter. I earned forty dollars a week. Forty dollars. And I was happy! I was happy because I thought of how many pesos it was. Forty dollars, and I didn't leave the house. I had nowhere to go. I sent money to my children and to pay my debts. I spent ten dollars, and I had thirty left to send and to save. By the time I left, I was getting seventy dollars per week.

My brother was in California, but I didn't go there because he did not like family members to come. He said we could suffer here or we could suffer at home.

But he went to Mexico and found out that I was in Texas. When he returned to California, he sent for me. He sent me the money to come here from Texas, so I got here. I had come for only a year, but I've been here for thirteen.

The Interview

I stayed with my brother's family for about a week—while I looked for a job. I found one through an interview in an agency. In Texas, I bought almost no clothes, because I wanted to save money. My sister-in-law's mother, who was about my size, let me borrow a dress so that I would be presentable for the interview. I went without breakfast.

I got to the agency and there were ten of us, Salvadoreans, some from Honduras, and Mexicans like me. I didn't know what was going on. I sat down next to them. My sister-in-law said that she would pick me up, that I should phone her when I was done. I expected to return to her house.

The first ones to arrive went in first. While I waited, the girls would come out and talk about the interview. I just listened.

Sara in her kitchen.

I was one of the last ones to go in. I saw them, and they looked at me. I sat down and they kept looking at me. They started to ask me questions—my name, if I had children, how many—and I would answer them. "Do you have small children?" "No," I said, "the youngest is ten." They asked a lot of questions. Probably because they wanted to see if you are telling the truth.

"Why did you come here?" Wow, I thought, If I tell them all my problems, the story will be very long. But the principal thing is money. He kept looking at me, and began to laugh, and said, "I'll tell you one of the things: the principal problem is money!" "That's it," I said. And she begins to laugh and says, "That's good." She asked if I liked children. I said, "Of course I do; I have four of my own. I love children. I'm here of necessity."

I think they could see that I was telling the truth, and the woman asked me, "How about the ten-year-old? How do you feel about leaving him?" I said, "Madam, don't ask me that. I'll cry right here." He said, "Right!" and they both began to laugh.

Then they told me what they needed and asked me why I had come from Texas. I told them my brother had sent for me to be here with him, and I told them that I would give them the phone number of the woman I worked for there, if they wanted it.

That was it. They had interviewed me. The secretary told me to sit down where I had been before. It was after noon, and it came down to a woman who spoke English and me.

The secretary came to get me and said, "Come. You will go with the couple." I thought, My God, I'm going to a strange house, and I don't even know where it is. One feels bad, disoriented. "Okay," I said, "Yes." And they took me back in to talk with the couple.

They said that I had impressed them, that I would go with them. "With pleasure," I said. "I'm really pleased that you picked me." And they had a three-month-old girl with them. When we were on the way out, I said, "May I take your baby? I'll take her right here."

Well, I worked for them for five years. I was with the little one every day. And they had another daughter who was three and a half. The little one was Gabriela and the other one, Andrea. They said they wanted me to stay with them, and I did. I took the children to school and took care of the house. It was my house too. They are Peruvians, so they talked with me in Spanish. They helped me a lot and still do. They were very nice with me.

With Gabriela and Andrea, the girls Sara cared for when she worked as a nanny/housekeeper (1993).

Bringing the Family

After I had been here for two years, I decided to go to Mexico. I had talked with them about my husband and everything. The man said, "Well, Sara, if you want to go, go. But I'll bring only your two sons for you." My oldest son had already come. And my daughter was married in Mexico. There were only the two younger sons, the eleven- and fourteen-year-olds. I was concerned about them. He said, "Look. Go. And bring your sons. You can put them in school here, and you will be less concerned, more tranquil."

So I went. They gave me three months of leave. But I didn't bring just my sons. I brought the whole family, including my husband, who my employer had said I should not bring. "Leave him," he said. "He didn't appreciate you. Leave him." But I was stubborn, foolish. I thought, How could the father of my children stay there? They would suffer. And it never crossed my mind to say, "I'm going to leave my husband"—even if he said things that hurt me. So, my husband came, my sons, even my son-in-law came. My daughter was pregnant and came later, after she gave birth. My employer helped us get an apartment. With my children here I was happy, content.

I put my youngest son in school. In the end he didn't graduate from high school. He lacked about two months,

and it was all because of one bad course. He didn't want to finish. And I said, "Well, that's it." If he doesn't want to, sometimes you can force a person, but if they don't want to, what do you do? Right?

I have four children, and, thank God, they all have jobs, not as professionals, but regular jobs. Two are car painters, and my daughter and the other son work in restaurants. I thank God that they are well, that they didn't turn to drugs, and that they don't have bad reputations. And I'm thankful for my work. Well, that's how my life is going.

Cleaning Houses

And here I am working as a housecleaner. The Peruvians I worked for treated me very well. I had to leave them because the children grew up.

I've been cleaning houses for seven or eight years; I don't like it so much because I have to deal with different people. Sometimes one of my daughters-in-law helps me, and when I had an operation a year ago, one of them did my work, and she met all of my employers. She said that when she went with me to the jobs, my employers were very nice to me. "Really," I said, "they do treat me well." I'm happy to

do the work because I have good employers. I said to her, "We come to do the work because they need it. I wouldn't like to work for a person who treated me badly—someone who saw me as a thing, as an animal, or that treated me badly." I would leave them, because I don't like to be treated badly.

When I go to do housecleaning, I respect everything.

That is what our parents taught us—to respect people, to respect another's things. My father used to say, "There's always room for honorable people, and those who are not are not welcome anywhere." And I think that's good advice. Even though we were poor, my father taught us to respect everything.

When her daughter, Leticia, has a free day, she helps Sara clean houses.

Her Husband Is Here

With my husband here the husband routine is back again. Sometimes I say, "Oh, my God, why did I bring him?" My daughter says, "You are very resentful with my dad. And that is why you cry." I cry because he was unfaithful to me. He went with another woman. I think I'm hurt because of this. When I came to the United States, he had been unfaithful to me in Mexico. I felt a strong urge to leave. "Yes, I'm going," I said to my friend. "Yes, I'm going to the United States"—because he had already done that to me. Maybe he did it because he did not love me anymore. When I told him I was leaving, he said, very happily, "Well, go ahead."

My daughter says, "You are being taught to forgive [in church], and that's what you should do." I tell her, "You forgive, but you don't forget!" And she says, "Mom, but when you pardon in your heart, you forget." And I say, "What a heart I have—that I can't forget."

The only thing that is not going well now is living with my husband. I don't know what is going on with us. Could it be him? Maybe it's because he drinks. Perhaps it will get better in the future. It's burdensome to have an alcoholic husband. I say he's alcoholic; he says he's not. What do you think if a person drinks every weekend and gets drunk? Isn't that alcoholism? My children tell me not to worry about it.

I forget for a minute, and the next minute it's back. For a while I forget it, and then I remember it again. It hurts me to say it, but I'm in this routine with him. Yesterday [a Friday] I did my work, and I went to some stores and walked around the street. I stopped by the beauty shop for my hair and got home about seven. My husband was there drinking. I didn't say anything to him, and he didn't say anything to me. I don't know what's going on. He doesn't even say, "Hi. Where did you go?" We live in this strange situation, and I don't like it. So I talk with my daughter. I let my children know what I am doing. I don't tell my husband.

I don't know how long I can stand this. It may end up the way it did when he was telling me that he was going to the United States. He kept saying, "I'm going to go. I'm going to go." And I didn't ever think of coming. Now it will be the same. He says that he is going, that he's going to Mexico—like a threat. But he doesn't go. I'll go! Maybe I'll beat him again!

The Wednesday prayer meeting at Sara's Catholic church is led by young people.

Prayer Meetings Help Her

Well, I'm going to the church prayer group, and I know what one should do. We study the Bible. Well, if I'm bad, maybe this is why I'm in this situation. But I thought about it, and, well, I did not cause the problem for him. Obviously, I'm not saying that I'm a saint. We all make mistakes. I don't know. Because I can't stand talking about him. I don't cry—but I always feel like crying when I talk about him.

The main thing is the husband, because we women follow the husband, right? What he teaches us about living,

or, how would I say it: I follow him. But they should be good examples, because if he is, for example, like mine, then I wouldn't follow him. I won't be like him.

So, at times I say to him, "You know what? The way you are bothers me!" "Are you sorry that you married me?" he says. "No, what bothers me is the way you are. It's, I don't know, your way of being." He says, "Did it take you until now to notice it?" I tell him, "I've always been aware of it." But how can I say it? It might be that he'll change. But look. It's been thirty-five years and he's still the same.

Sara dancing at the meeting.

Sara's son-in-law, Victor Cienfuegos (center), is one of the men who take collections and assist with the meeting.

And my daughter tells to me bear with it. I say to her, "Well, what do you want me to do? When I was married, they told me, 'Until death do us part!'" Imagine that. And I tell her, "So death will separate us." She says, "And now that you are having a hard life?" And I tell her, "What do you want? What do you want me to say to your father?" "Well, get divorced" [she says]. I tell her, "Well, these days people divorce, but to those extremes I won't go. I will not divorce," I say. "If your father wants to leave, let him go. I'm doing fine here." I will keep working at my job, very tranquilly. "May he not annoy me," I tell her—because now I will not let him bother me. And that's it. Because what can I do? Now he can do whatever he wants to. She says, "You could remedy a lot of things." I tell her, "That's exactly why I go to church—to become calmer."

Before, if my husband had words with me, I answered badly. But now I attend the prayer meeting and it makes me calmer. There I'm well, and I'll keep going to them. Someday you could go there to see how we do it—if you would like to.

I don't know if what I've said will help you, but everything I said has happened to me. It is all true.

Tina Parker was born and raised in Orange County. Her family includes her daughters, Amanda and Ashley, her husband, Chris Smith, and their son, Parker. They rent a suburban house in northern Orange County. It is about twenty miles from many of the houses she and her assistant clean.

Tina Parker

My life story would begin actually when I was in the third grade. I'm going way back. I have to go way back for you to understand where I am and how I've gotten to where I am today. When I was in the third grade, I had just started, my mother decided due to her religion that I didn't need an education, because I wouldn't be sitting here today. The world was going to come to an end. I'm thirty now. She did not believe I would ever be thirty in this world. So an education was unnecessary. So, in the beginning of my third-grade year, she took me out of school, and she took my brother and my sister out and decided she would teach us at home—which lasted maybe, at the most, three months. Amongst her attempts to teach us at home, she obviously had us going into her religion and knocking on doors—she was a Jehovah's Witness knocking on doors, doing all the Bible stuff. That was the only thing we were allowed to do as children.

But then when I grew, I was twelve, she decided that I didn't have anything to do with myself—which was true because I didn't attend school, she did not believe in sports, she did not believe in having associates outside of the religion. So we weren't really allowed to associate with anybody in the neighborhood. All we were really allowed to do was go knock on doors and preach my mother's religion.

She decided when I was twelve that I should start working. She did housecleaning for a living—with my grandmother. So she started me out doing small things here and there; whatever you could do at the age of twelve. So basically I have been doing this for eighteen years because I've been doing it since I was twelve. People don't believe it because they look at me and go, "You're too young to have been cleaning houses for eighteen years," but I have been.

So I guess I do what I do now because it's the only thing that I've ever done in my entire life. It's all I know, and to go off and get a job right now is impossible for me. What do I put down on a form, that I've only completed third grade? It's not going to get you a job. Not that I haven't had jobs outside of housecleaning, because I have, but I guess I found that the money is better in housecleaning than it is anywhere else.

I don't know what else you want me to say because that's where I am right now in my life because of that. I think I do what I do now because I'm able to be with my kids and I'm able to make my own hours and I make whatever income I want to make. It has its pluses and its drawbacks, but I think I'm still doing what I'm doing right now because I have had my kids at the age that I had them at and I guess it's best for our family right now.

FC: *How about the rest of your life?*

I was thinking about this the other day—what I would say about my life. My entire life has been nothing but work. In fact, for the first time Thursday, I got out of bed and said, "You know what? I just can't go to work today. I just can't." That was the first time. I mean, yes, I have had days that I've missed because maybe my kids are sick or something, but it was the first time that I personally, myself, said, "I cannot go to work today. I am tired. I need to stay in bed." And I did it. I mean, I don't even take vacation times. I rarely ever take time off. So for the last—and it's not a joke—for the last eighteen years I have done nothing but housecleaning and raising my kids. That's it. I'm serious. I'm not kidding you, Frank, I'm not kidding. I mean, when I think about talking about my life, my life is my work. That's it. My work and then my kids. That's all I do. So my entire life is what time am I going to pick my son up, what time he's going to go to karate, what time I'm going to pick Ashley up, what time she's going to go to soccer, what time I'm going to pick Amanda up, and

she's going to go to dance. I personally don't really have a life outside of my kids. That's all I have to say because that's my life. I'm serious. I'm really serious. That's it.

Schooling

I'm the youngest. She took us all out of school. My sister went back to school and she became a schoolteacher, which I think is awesome. That's great. And my brother, I don't think he ever went back to school and he has his own business too. That's what you do. But we all three of us went into my mom's cleaning business and helped her out with it. We all did. And I think there should be a law against that [*little laugh*]. I think there is one. I hope there would be one. I always wondered why nobody ever stepped in and did anything.

It was new fad, or whatever, to teach your kids at home, and so I guess people didn't pay attention to it. People were just starting to do it.

My mom turned one of the rooms of our home into a school, but she was so busy Bible-thumping, is what I like to say, that it just kind of faded away. The first couple of weeks, I'd say, we used to get out of bed on time, and we'd sit there and do our thing. And then, well, like I said, it just slowly faded away. No longer did the alarm go off to get up.

She felt that we would learn to read through going to church, which is true—we did. I'm a great reader.

Tina in her living room.

I can read probably better than most people can because I can read the Bible. I actually have a lot of education from the Bible stuff, but nothing of the social part of it—learning to interact with people. I think that did more harm to me than the actual not sitting down learning to do math.

FC: *What did you do all day?*
Exactly! What did I do all day? Thank you! That's why she put me to work at the age of twelve. Because I didn't have anything to do with myself. We would go to church and we would go door-to-door like they do. And then what did I do for the rest of the day? I sat in my room. I stayed home. Because I wasn't allowed to have friends. I found trouble. I found something to do.

From Mother to Chris

FC: *Well, there must have been a moment when you left your mother's house.*
When I was twenty-one. I had just had Ashley, I think.

We had moved to Ireland for two years because of my mother's religion. I didn't want to go. I kicked and clawed and she made me go. Of course then it was the happiest thing that ever happened to me and I was totally thrilled. I loved it there, and I would live there today if I could. It's just a beautiful place to live. I would love to go back there.

She hated it. She wanted to come back. I didn't want to come back. I kicked and fought not to come back and she decided that because I couldn't get a visa to work there that I had to come back with her. Of course I got the visa to work like a month after I moved back here. They sent it to me in the mail.

FC: *How old were you then, when you came back?*
I was twenty. So I moved out of my mom's house when I was twenty-one, and that's when I started doing house-cleaning on my own. I picked up all the jobs that I had left when I moved to Ireland. I picked them all up again. I decided that I was going to just work my butt off and work as hard as I possibly could just so I didn't have to live at home, because I didn't like it [*laughs*]. Because I didn't believe in things my mother did, and I just needed out of it. It was basically, "You live in my house, you're going to follow these religious rules." I could have gone back to school, but I would have had to have done it living in my mom's house, which would have meant that my kids would have been raised pretty much in the same exact way that I was raised, except that they probably would have gone to school. I would have made sure of that.

But I just said, "You know what, I can't do this for myself or my kids anymore"—so I just worked my butt off. And I worked hard to get to where I am today and to have the referrals I have today. I used to work from six in the morning to six at night, sometimes seven o'clock at night. I still remember this one time I worked from six in the morning to nine o'clock at night. Just a lot of hard work is what my life has been.

FC: *So at some point you met Chris.*
Mm-hmm [yes]. I met Chris in nineteen—oh, when did I meet Chris?—nineteen ninety-three. I had just moved out, pretty much, and met him one night and he moved in the next day and that was that. That was it. Basically he came and stayed and never went home. We laugh about that. We totally laugh about that. That's it!

So now my life ever since has been being married and having kids. 'Cause once you have a family, isn't that all your life's about is kids?

My mom and dad were divorced when I wasn't even born. I was raised by my mom. They were divorced over the religion.

My dad wasn't in my life as a child. When I was—I can't remember how old I was, maybe eleven or something—my mom decided that we weren't going to see him anymore due to her religion, so he dropped out of our lives until I became, gosh, until I married Chris, and Chris got me back into seeing him again. So he's just now come back into my life, maybe three years ago. So now I've gone from not talking to my dad to talking to my dad and not talking to my mom.

Why I Am Shy

I think that what has happened is because I missed out on the social part of going to school—isn't that where you make your friends, you learn to interact with people, you get self-confidence? All of those things I missed out on. So I'm an extremely shy person. I'm very quiet. I stay home. I don't do anything, because that's what I've known for my entire life. Even when I was a kid, my mom didn't even let me out of the house to spend the night at a friend's house. I stayed home all the time and did nothing. And I think I'm doing the same thing as an adult but making sure that my kids don't live like that, making sure that they have everything that I did not as a kid. So I spend 24/7 making sure that they are taken care of and have all that extra sports and fun that I didn't have as a kid. And that is my life. That's it. It's nice and boring. It's exactly what I said to Chris the other day. I said, "Chris, you know what? I am like so boring. I really am. I'm quiet and I haven't really done that much in my life." And I think it's due to my mother's upbringing of me—which makes sense. So that's that, Frank.

I work. I meet great people. I mean, I'm thankful for my work because I like to say I make my own hours, but I really don't make my own hours anymore. Once you get the business as built up as mine is, you better be at work at this time so that you can be picking your kids up at this time. So I say I have the drawbacks. I meet a lot of people. I meet my clients, but it's not the interaction that you would have if you have a normal job—I'd like a normal job.

FC: What's a normal job?

Exactly. What's a normal job? Where you have people you work with every day, you get to know them, you hang out with them, they become your friends. I don't have that. I just have acquaintances that I meet, and okay. So I kind of miss that, not having the interaction with people. But then, I've met a lot of extremely nice people and people that I've worked for forever, and I become part of the family. So that's always nice.

But I'm not normal, I think. I'm not normal like most people who have had schooling and have gone on to college and have gone on to try jobs and all this stuff. To me, it was just like, here you're twelve, this is what you're doing, and you do it until now.

And I see myself doing it until the kids are gone. Because what job's going to give me the money I make? I make really good money. Especially for somebody who's had a third-grade education. I'm not going to be able to walk into anyplace and make the money I make. So if I have to thank my mother for anything, I'll thank her for that.

But then most people will say to me, why don't you go back to school? When? Would that be after I get home at six o'clock and I've made dinner and did the bath and did the story time and put my son to bed at eight? Exactly when would I be going back to school? And that's not fair to me, that's not fair to my kids to take that time, that little time I do have with them.

Parker's fourth birthday party.

Parker raises his hand to answer the hired Batman's question.

The cake. Amanda (left) and Ashley, wearing the balloon crowns.

Grandparents

FC: *That's it. I know, but we still have tape left. Let's pause and see if it inspires. . . . I have an idea. Do me a favor. Pick some little thing in your life and describe it in detail.*

My favorite memory I have in life is my grandfather [father's father] coming to pick us up every other weekend. He would ring the doorbell, he would have his little—we would open up the door and he would have his little hello charm—he'd go, "*Hello,*" in that tone every single time, and he would say the same exact thing, "We missed you. You guys ready to have a great weekend?" And off we would go with him, and I'd get into his big blue car and buckle up and I'd be in front with him and his lunchbox would be to my left and he'd push it over to me and he would say, "You know, today I just didn't feel like eating that Twinkie, I saved it, so you can have it." And now I look back at that as an adult and I think: It just happened that every other Friday he just didn't feel like having his Twinkie?

He would take us to the grocery store right away, and we all used to be able to just pile everything into the cart that we wanted, and off to his house we would go. And my grandmother would be there, with her open arms and hugs and kisses for us when we showed up, and my brother would go to the TV room; I would go to the picture room and look through all the pictures as a kid—that was my big thing—it still is, and that is my best memory, going to my grandparents' home. Because we were able to be who we were—we were able to just kind of relax when we were there, you know. There was no Bible reading going on. We used to

get to watch as much TV as we wanted, which wasn't something we could do at home. I think that's all we ever did. We ate and watched TV the entire time. And they let us. That's all—"You know what, whatever you guys want to do, you can do it"—and that's what we did.

It was my father's weekend, but my grandfather would pick us up, and we would stay with my grandmother. I mean, my dad would pop in. It was more like it was my grandparents' every other weekend than it was my dad's. And just having the smell of my grandmother constantly cooking in the kitchen, and after we had shoved ourselves full of junk food galore, she would have made this spread of dinner for us, and we would all sit there and look at it and go, "Oh God, we're so full," but we would sit there and we would shove ourselves full of more food. We used to come back just rolling, we were so full. We just couldn't wait to get back there. So that's my best memory.

My mother didn't celebrate holiday time, and so when our birthdays would come around or Christmas would come around, they would buy us things but make sure that it wasn't done on our exact birthday or exact Christmas Day. I was just looking at pictures the other day, and all of our Christmas presents were wrapped in—our so-called Christmas presents, they were called love gifts—they were wrapped in newspaper, because we weren't allowed to have Christmas wrapping. But they still—my grandparents and my dad—tried to give us that memory as a kid. So that was always fun.

And we used to sit back and watch my family decorate a Christmas tree because we weren't allowed to.

It was so funny, though, as a child, you do what you want to do when you know the other parent's not around, so I still remember my brother, he walked up and took a piece of Christmas tinsel and walked up and put it on the tree, and I'm like younger than he is, I'm sitting there going, "Oh, you're so busted." So of course the first thing I do when I get home to my mom—"Mom, you know what Scott did?"

FC: *[laughs]*

Exactly. Poor kid. Of course I apologize now for that, but I remember it. It was something so silly, just putting a piece of tinsel on a tree.

My brother is two years older and my sister is four years older. I'm the baby. That's why when my grandfather died this year, it was really hard.

Yeah. I lost three relatives this year—my grandmother [mother's mother] died in March, my mother-in-law died in May, and my grandfather just died on September seventeenth. I never lost anybody in my life, and it was like one after another this year. It's been a yucky year.

It was nice this last Christmas—I had my grandfather and my mother-in-law both at my home for Christmas. It was the first Christmas I had ever had at my house, and they both were there.

This Christmas will be hard. But it'll be fun. Of course that's one thing I think my childhood has done for me.

Tina with her grandfather (1999).

I love the holidays now. And I just go all out for my kids for holidays and make sure everything's perfect. Of course I stress myself out unbelievably.

That was a nice memory to have. Thank you.

Leidi Mejia has two daughters. The older one was born in Guatemala in the late 1970s. She now is married and lives with her husband and three children in a nearby Orange County city. Monica, Leidi's younger daughter, was born in California in 1994. Leidi and Monica share an apartment with Leidi's nephew, Gabriel Ramirez.

Leidi's sister, Esperanza, who lives about two blocks away, is also a housecleaner. She tells her story in a later chapter. Leidi and Esperanza have a brother, who lives and works in Southern California, and five sisters. Four live in Guatemala, one in the United States.

Leidi Mejia

My name is Leidi Mejia. I'm forty-eight years old. I was born in Guatemala of Guatemalan parents, Gabriel Mejia and Carmen Villafuerte. I come from a large family: seven girls and one boy. My parents were in a very tight economic situation. My father worked. My mother made bread to sell. But we were happy, a very large and unified family. We had plenty to eat. Like all families, the children fought. There are always some people more mischievous than others.

I had the best parents in the world. If I were to be born again, I would choose the same parents. My father was a very picky, very clean person. So was my mother. And they raised us to be honest people, and clean. And I grew up with that orientation—that of honesty and cleanliness as very important in a person's life.

We had a school near my father and my mother. It was a very small school, and it didn't have enough room for many children, so the older ones went. My sister Telma, my sister Yoly, and my sister Mirza were all in school.

When they came back from school, I would write, and look at their homework and help them. When there was room for me in the school, in first grade, I was seven, and I knew how to read and write and add and subtract—everything. The teacher gave me an exam to evaluate my work and passed me into the second grade. I did well because I was always trying to learn—to learn more and more. It seemed easy for me. So I grew and I finished secondary school.

My father didn't have money to send all of us to the university. Neither did my mother. So we got together one night, and they said, "Okay, only one will be able to go to the university." Esperanza was there. Luis was there. The others did well, but not well enough to go to the university. So I said, "Okay, I want to go. I want to be somebody; I want to be a teacher, I want to be a nurse, I want to be a doctor, I want to study." And my mother and my father said, "You know what, daughter? Your brother is also very intelligent.

Leidi's parents (1973).

Here we can only send one." Then my brother said, "Give me the opportunity. You are women. You will probably fall in love and get married, and I'm a man. For women it is more difficult." Well, Esperanza and Telma and I started to talk about it. "What will we do?" And he said, "I want to study. I want to study." And it was true, he was very intelligent. He had very good grades. Then we agreed, "Okay, we will give you the opportunity to go to the university, to Peten Poptún."

So he began—and we looked for work. We worked and helped our mother. At that time I was fifteen years old. I began working at the Bandegua Company. We packed bananas for export to Europe. I began with a job that wasn't heavy. It was checking the quality of production. That was the work that they gave to people who had more schooling. I worked there for about five years. When I got my pay, every two weeks, I would give it to my mother. She would buy me clothes and everything that I needed.

Her Husband

When I was nineteen, I met the man who became my first husband. He proposed, and we were engaged for seven years. Then we decided to get married and go to Guatemala City, because we were living in a small town. My mother was very sad, but I said to her, "Don't worry. I won't forget you."

The idea was to go to the capital and to continue studying. But unfortunately, my husband was very egotistical. He wanted his wife in his house. He didn't want someone who wanted to advance. I said to him, "It can't be that way. I want a family, but I also want to help. I am going to work; I'm going to study. Now I don't have children. I can do it." He was a policeman there. I began to work in a supermarket as a cashier. I finished a course for a nurse's assistant. It wasn't very much, but it was something that could help me in the future. Later I left that supermarket, and I went to a pharmacy. I learned a lot in the pharmacy.

After we had been married about two years, he decided he wanted to go to the United States—supposedly to make a better life. I had a daughter who was one year old. I said, "Okay." He went.

Three months later he came back, despondent, saying that life was very hard without a family. Later he said, "If we could go together, it might be better, because we would be together, and we could support each other. You can send your mother money from there." I said, "Okay." It was 1979, February of 1979. It was very hard to leave my country. It was very hard to leave my daughter. I left her with my sister Esperanza.

Her First Trip to the United States

We got to Tijuana. There they took us to another person and then to the road to the border crossing. I almost died—a car almost ran me over. My husband really wanted to get into the United States. He went ahead and left me alone to cross the freeway when they tell you "cross!" over to the other side. I fell and cut my knees. I kept walking with my knees bleeding—in the dark, with lots of spines and mud—until we reached some houses. I think that was San Diego. They took us to a house where there were a lot of people and gave us cooked potatoes to eat. In the morning they put us in the trunk of a car, five people in the car trunk. We felt we would suffocate. They took us to another house. I had only the clothes I had on—all the rest were left along the road. I washed my clothes at night and put them on the next day, still wet.

The day after she arrived in Los Angeles (near Figueroa and Pico) Leidi had a job ironing blouses in a garment factory— for two cents each. She worked there about a month. Over the next ten months she had three other jobs. To avoid a living situation where there was a lot of drinking, she worked as a live-in housekeeper for an elderly man for two weeks. Then for three months she glued insoles into shoes—for fifty cents each. And finally she worked for seven months in another garment factory. There she began trimming loose threads from finished garments at five cents each and, after a week, was made an inspector of finished jackets.

At this time my husband met a Salvadoran woman where he worked. She was about fifty. He was about thirty-two. This woman fell in love with him and, I think, he with her. And she said to him, "Divorce your wife, marry me—I'll get you papers." He began to have a relationship with this woman.

I noticed. When we were married, I told him, "I like honest people. I like fidelity. I don't like treachery. I can stand hunger, poverty, cold, but no blows and no treachery." That was our understanding.

When I realized that he was going out with her, she began calling me on the phone—that they saw each other at the office, and there they had their things. And then I told her that that didn't interest me, that I was the wife and that I wasn't going to see anything at the office. Finally the moment arrived when I said to him, "You know what, if you don't love me anymore, then let's get divorced and you can go on with your life." He said, "I only want to get papers. Let's get divorced, and I'll go get married with her. I'll get my papers, and then I'll divorce her and I'll get papers for you." I told him, "No. This is not going to happen."

Her Second Trip to the United States

Leidi separated from her husband and returned to Guatemala, planning to stay there, but decided to return to the United States, where she could make more money. She brought her daughter and her mother with her. They arrived at a friend's house. She soon found a small apartment and met a woman who wanted a housekeeper.

It was already easier. I had a notion of how to work in an American house. I worked for her for a year very hard— from six in the morning until ten at night. She paid me a salary of $125 per week. Saturday and Sunday, I worked cleaning the house of a friend of hers—and was making a total of about $160 week. With this I paid the rent and helped my mother to maintain my household. I continued to meet more people—with the help of Leslie O'Rourke, the first person who gave me a house to clean when I arrived.

After two or three years I had my five houses for the week. They paid me fifty dollars per day. For me it was a lot of money at that time—more or less 1984 and 1985. Life was very good here. It wasn't very expensive then.

Her Third Trip to the United States

After a year in the United States, Leidi's mother returned to Guatemala. Leidi, feeling lonely in the United States with her daughter, followed and tried to establish herself in Guatemala. She watched her savings go down and decided to return to the United States, where she began a long period of work to establish an independent household with her daughter. Her husband did not help them, and later, with the help of an employer who was a lawyer, she got a divorce. During this period she tried to create a larger family by helping many of her close relatives, including her sister Esperanza, to come to the United States.

Frank, I worked six days a week, from eight in the morning to five, six in the afternoon. And honestly, it was a very hard battle, a hard fight for me because I didn't control English,

Leidi and her younger daughter, Monica, in their living room. Photos of Monica and certificates and medals from her elementary school and tae kwon do classes decorate the wall.

From the outset Leidi wanted my pictures to feature Monica. One weekend I went to Leidi's house to deliver some pictures and found her with a sister and brother-in-law visiting from Guatemala and other relatives from Los Angeles. They urged Leidi to be the one featured, but she insisted that it be Monica. Monica enters Leidi's story toward the end of this chapter.

I never went to school because I had obligations, I was a single mother. I was responsible for a little girl. And my daughter began to go to school. Someone picked her up for me. Later I passed by and got her. At that time I didn't drive; I rode the buses. I had to get up very early, at four thirty in the morning, to take a bath and prepare my daughter. I had to take the bus at 6:30 or 7:00 a.m. in order to arrive at 8:00, 8:30 at my jobs, because—despite having my own, let's say my own business, my houses—I always liked to be responsible, to put myself on a schedule.

My [first] daughter was growing and I was working at the same thing. I gave my daughter everything I did not have as a child—toys, the brand-name clothes that she liked. I tried to give her good food, good examples. It was a very hard life for me—of aloneness and struggle—but I'm proud of that. My daughter finished primary school and began what here is called high school. And that's when my sadness, my struggle, began.

When she began to go to high school and have friends, I don't know what happened, but rebellion began. She fought with me a lot. She was ashamed that I was a housekeeper—or housecleaner, as they say. I wasn't ashamed of it. It's an honest job; it's a decent job with which I brought her up. And I'm now bringing up my second daughter [Monica].

Leidi Goes to Night School

Leidi found a cosmetology program and qualified for a scholarship at Rancho Santiago, a community college (now Santa Ana College).

I spoke to the people where I worked and told them I needed to leave a little earlier because I was going to study. Many of them said, "Why are you going to do it? You don't have to do that. You're making very good money here with us." But I'm not always going to clean houses. I need to do something that I like. I'm not saying that I don't like to clean houses. I don't like it, but neither do I say I'm not going to do it. It's a job and I take it. I have taken it as a job like any other.

The teacher said to me, "Here all the classes are in English. There is no Spanish. I said, "Don't worry. I'm going to memorize the words in English." Frank, I arrived at home dead tired. My daughter was thirteen years old. I knew that she could take care of herself. I picked her up; I left her at my house; I made dinner for her; I went to school. I returned home after school at about twelve thirty in the morning.

Learning to Drive

One night I was waiting for the bus to go home, and some gang kids passed. They asked me for money and I didn't

Monica (center) with her tae kwon do class.

give them any. And they hit me and grabbed my books. A lady passing in a car said to me, "Get in. If you stay here, they'll kill you." They threw a rock at her and broke one of the windows of her car. She left me at my house.

I said, "I have to drive." That was Thursday. On Saturday, I spoke with a friend and said, "Guess what? I have five hundred dollars and I want to buy a car." He said, "What?" "Yes," I said, "I'm going to buy a used car, any kind. I'm going to drive." "Oh," he said. "Great! Let's go!"

He took me to Harbor Boulevard in Santa Ana and bought me a four-hundred-dollar car. I didn't know how to drive. He half explained it to me. Move this, push there, and you're all set. And he said, "Okay. Here is your car. Go to your house." I got in the car. My legs were shaking, and he said to me, "Go to your house."

I got to my house. Thank God nothing happened to me on the way. People were blowing their horns at me, shouting at me, and I didn't know what I was doing, but I got there. I got in the car again and followed the bus that went to where I was working. I went behind the bus. At the end of the week I was shaking. I had a horrible fear and was telling myself, "I could crash into someone. Someone could hit me, and I'm going to die."

I stopped driving. I told my friend, "You know what? Take the car, because I'm afraid." He said, "No. You are going to drive." I said, "I don't have—" "You drove for a week. You're going to drive. Nothing happened to you. You're not afraid. You just have to be careful."

I hadn't read the book; I hadn't gotten a license; I hadn't done anything. I didn't drive for a week. The next week I said, "No. I am going to drive." And I got in the car again and began. That's how it went. A month passed. Two months passed. Things went well. Later I went to get the book. I read it. And I went to get my license, and I passed. With my license I felt better. I kept that car.

School

I continued in school. I studied for a year and a half, from five in the afternoon to ten at night. On Saturdays, I went from eight in the morning to five in the afternoon—all day. It was hard but not impossible because I wanted to do it, and every weekend I sat down to memorize the words in English for the next exam.

And let me say that all my exams were ninety and one hundred! Once the teacher said to me, "You're copying someone." I had a Mexican teacher. It seemed that she didn't like me, because she even ordered me to change my uniform, because I had bought tight Levi's, like the ones I'm wearing now, and a white blouse, and she told me that she didn't want this, that she wanted loose pants.

"That's good," I said. "I'll put on loose pants, if that's what you want." I bought loose pants and put on the uniform that the teacher wanted. "Are you happy?" I said to her.

In class, there were those who really took the class and those that didn't. You know how it is here: nobody is obligated. People would go out for a smoke, or they would say, "Let's go have a drink." I would say, "No. I'm going to study. You go. Tell me about it later."

I had only one friend, a little Chinese man. He was very interested in the work, like me. He was the only one that followed me. In the break we would read. He also had very bad English, but he really wanted to learn and to get a license. When there were the semester exams everybody would sit with us so they could copy and pass the exam.

Once when we were doing a midyear exam, the teacher said to me, "You're not going to pass." And I said, "Yes, I will pass, because I studied. I'm going to get a hundred." When she graded the exams, I had a hundred. She called me and said, "You didn't do this alone." And I said, "Then who helped me? Give me an exam—whatever exam you want (because there were four exams). Give it to me and put me in the bathroom alone. But you know what? I will pass this test, and I want to speak with the director, because you are harassing me a lot." That's how she gave me the exam. She put me in the bathroom, and I said, "Give me ten minutes to do the exam." When I gave her the completed new form of the exam, she said, "Let me

make sure you don't have a cheat sheet." "Whatever you like," I said, "but if you take off my clothes, you are going to have problems, because you are accusing me of something that is not true. Call the director." And they called the director. I said to him, "This woman is harassing me a lot. I was afraid to complain, but she was really doing a lot to me. And now she wants to check my body to see if I have a cheat sheet. Call a girl to check me."

I showed him the two exams. He congratulated me and thanked me for having told him what the teacher was doing with me. He said that she would not bother me again, that if she did, she would have to leave the school, because she had to respect her students. After that she changed a lot. She apologized. She said, "You seem to me to be a very creative person, one who can do anything." And I said to her, "No, I want to do this very much."

Finally the moment of my graduation arrived. It was a very emotional moment. I had all my family there, many friends; I have videos; I have photos.

After the graduation I had to do three months of study in order to prepare for my license exam. I memorized that book from head to toe, word for word. I said, "I'm going to get my license." My English wasn't very good, but with a lot of memorizing I read English. I had many, many problems with pronunciation.

I arrived at the exam very nervous. A friend took me to the exam, a very nice lady who supported me a lot.

Luz Stuart is her name. She was my client from the beginning, and she was my model, because you have to bring to the exam a model to do the work on. We woke up very early, five in the morning, in order to get to the exam in Los Angeles at seven. I arrived at the exam with a very positive attitude. There were about eighty of us taking the exam. The exam lasted for six hours. First the practice, later the written part. There were two hundred written questions, and I said, "I know this by memory, by rote." When they give a recess so as to calculate the results to see if you passed and get your license, I said, "My God, what's going to happen?"

I knew that it would be yes, and they began to call the persons' names. Out of eighty people, seven passed. They called number two, number three, number four, and my name didn't come out. Number five and I said, "My God, I'm not going to make it." Number six, nothing. Then they said, "Number seven, Leidi Mejia." "Oh my God!" and they told me, "Your license will arrive by mail." I went to my house with the woman who accompanied me to the exam and she said, "Let's go celebrate." She invited me to drink a glass of champagne in a very nice place. My mother was here because at that time my mother had a visa and came to visit me every year. I brought her here every year. I said to my mother, "Mother, I'm going to dedicate my license to you. This is going to be my gift."

On Mondays, Wednesdays, and Fridays, Leidi goes with Monica to her 7 p.m. class near their home. She usually sits with her sister Esperanza, whose son is also in the class. Exams and awards ceremonies often happen on weekend afternoons.

Her Older Daughter Rebels

Soon serious problems with my daughter began, because I was working Saturday and Sunday in the salon. She had more liberty to have friends, and she began to rebel very seriously. I was raised in a different way—with roots and customs different from this country. I guess I never realized that the life and customs of every country are different. I didn't give her permission when she wanted to go to sleep at the house of her friends because I had noticed in some of my jobs what happened when girls got together to sleep at another house. Sex began, marijuana began, and things, if you understand me. I love my daughter and I didn't want her to lose herself. I wanted the best for her.

The troubles with her daughter continued. They had joint psychological counseling, and her daughter lived in foster homes for more than a year. She returned to live with Leidi about two months before her eighteenth birthday and left when she turned eighteen.

During this time I met a man at the salon where I was working. I was very depressed. I was very sad. I know that this is not a justification, but this person arrived in my life at a moment in which I was very desperate. He tried to be my friend, and soon he began to woo me. I liked him. He was, it seemed, a good person, and we began to go out, and I felt his moral support, that I wasn't alone, that I had someone who would give me love and give me protection, supposedly. At the beginning, everything was very nice.

Monica Is Born

For about a year, my relationship with him was growing. We loved each other. I fell in love with him. Supposedly he loved me a lot. We came to a relationship. We decided to live together as a couple, and from this a pregnancy resulted. When my stomach grew with my pregnancy, the man changed. It was like the love had ended. I was very occupied. I worked a lot. I had lots of problems, lots of sadness. When I realized I was pregnant, it was very sad for me. Then he began to want to go to parties and he didn't take me. I started to lose my figure. And because this bothered him that I was losing my figure, he left my house. I remained alone again, pregnant.

I began to struggle. I worked pregnant and kept going. I said, "This can't be, this can't be. I've got to begin again." I became very attached to this baby that I was awaiting. I had all my checkups. I took care of myself very well. I ate very well, and I knew that it was going to be another girl. I wanted a boy. I always wanted a boy. I had another girl. I was very, very sad, but I said, "It is my daughter, and God knows why He sent me another daughter." Frank, I worked a week before the birth. My stomach was enormous, enormous. I had a lot of problems. The baby moved a lot in my stomach. My skin hurt a lot. A lot of people said to me, "Now, don't come to work because I'm afraid that you'll have an accident," and I would say to them, "I'm fine." Physically I felt very well. I didn't have any problems with nausea or other problems with pregnancy—nothing. I had a lot of energy, and I attached myself to that child that I was waiting for.

Time passed. The birth of my daughter was approaching. My mother came to stay with me. She was with me when I gave birth because I had no one. All the relatives I helped to come here had taken up different lives—if you understand me. Each one lived a life. I accept and respect this. I said to myself, "It doesn't matter. I'm alone again and I will continue to battle." My daughter was born very healthy and strong. Her father did not want to give her his name. Later he came to see her, but he didn't want to pay child support—because, to this day, he doesn't want responsibilities. I have worked and struggled very hard, very hard. It was a moment when life was difficult.

Monica wins a medal.

Leidi with her mother (1992).

After Monica was born, my mother left. There I was, a single mother again. But it was different. I considered myself a part of California, where I live very well. I have grown economically. I had a license, a profession. I had matured a lot, Frank. I had fallen many times. Many times. I was humiliated many times in some of my jobs, but all that made me mature. I think I'm an honest and a good person. I'm not a bad person. And I think I'm a very lucky person as well. Very lucky because I have met two or three people who were very good with me. They have been like angels for me. All thanks to, who knows, the blessings of my mother and of God. I have had a very hard life, but I never got involved with drugs or prostitution, and I never will, because my parents taught me to fight, to be honest, to be a hard worker, and I will continue that way as long as my body permits me.

And I tell you, it was hard to begin again, like when I was a single mother the first time with my older daughter, now I am a single mother with Monica. Monica is a very active child, very endearing, and when she wants something, she gets it. I like that, I like her because if we set a goal—I have set very small goals for my daughter— she reaches them. I'm teaching her that "where there's a will, there's a way." And in this life one has to fight hard, not look for the easy way out.

I was pleased to be invited to the 2001 Christmas party at Leidi's home. Others present were Leidi, Monica, and Leidi's nephew, Gabriel Ramirez (the residents of the apartment); Leidi's sister Esperanza, her son, her boyfriend, her daughter, and her daughter's boyfriend; Leidi's older daughter, her husband, their three children, her husband's mother and younger brother; and Monica's father.

Gabriel (the manager of a catering business) produced an elegantly set table and a fine holiday meal.

Esperanza's boyfriend said grace in English, and Gabriel translated it into Spanish for those who were not bilingual.

Toward the end of dinner Esperanza's boyfriend rose to speak again. He announced their engagement. Gabriel presented a special bottle of wine, and there were toasts and talk, many pictures were taken, and Esperanza's daughter and her boyfriend were induced to reveal that they too had intentions.

After dessert, as the children tired, Leidi's older daughter, her family group, and Monica's father left.

Presents were opened a little early, and there was a champagne toast at midnight.

Leidi with Monica

And now I'm waiting. I'm sad. I'm alone. I have emptiness inside. For me the hardest thing in my life has been the loss of my mother. That hurt me very much. Today is the third anniversary of her death. It was something that, I don't know, hit me very hard. It stopped me. I felt her illness. Despite the distance that separated us, I always had good communication with her. I always thought of her as very important in my life—like moral support. When my father died, it hurt me very much, but my mother's death was harder. And I think, "Okay, today I have nothing. I have no father. I have no mother. My older daughter has left. I'm alone again."

When they first came to California in 1973, Victoria Rua and her husband left their two children in Mexico. Since then she has lived and worked here most of the time, while he has spent much of the time in Mexico. She is now here without him. She recently has lived with a relative's family and in different rented rooms in central Orange County. Her brother and her son also live in Southern California with their families.

Victoria Rua

My life has been sad because I lost my mother when I was nine years old. She died. I was left with only my father and a brother. It was a battle, because my father liked to drink a lot, and he was not, may he rest in peace, responsible with his family. He just thought of his vices and his friends and didn't take us into account. The neighbors always pitied us, my brother and me. We did what we could to help out—to earn our tortillas, at least a meal every day. Lately I miss my father. Well, bad or good, however he was, I still miss him. After I married, I took in my father. I had him with me always, until God took him. But, well, now I don't have many feelings about those things. They are things that do happen. At the same time they are sad.

A Short Overview

For a while I was with my father. After being with my father I was with a godmother—at the age of nine or ten. When I was fourteen, I went with my aunt. After that I was here and there, in one place and another, and then I got a boyfriend.

I didn't have a fifteenth-birthday ceremony (*quinceañera*). I didn't know when I was fifteen. I was, well, just living in the world. I didn't know who I was, how I was.

I went to school for a while, but my father soon took me out to make his tortillas—to wash and iron for him. I didn't have a chance to go to school. They reprimanded me because I didn't bring the right supplies. I was ashamed and I didn't go to school. I just stayed home and took care of things.

Then I got married and went to a farm. I got married because I suffered a lot with my father, and I thought that if I married, I would suffer less. So I married, and it was worse—because it wasn't the way I thought—that I would enjoy something different. It was worse, and then the children came, and I suffered with them. It was a very, very sad life for me. First I suffered with my father, because he liked to drink a lot. I got married and it was the same.

Then, with the help of a *comadre* [her daughter's godmother] who wanted us to come here, we both came here [in 1973]. I crossed first, and there was a problem about that. The people who helped my husband to cross

Victoria's sleeping mat and shoes at her father's
house in Tuxpan, Jalisco, Mexico (1982).

told him stories about what happened to women in
crossing, and he thought it happened to me too. He got
angry with me. He left and went back to Mexico.

I worked for a long time. I worked as a live-in for three
years, and then I left and got a job in a factory. I didn't get
along with the people there. There was lots of envy, lots of
problems, and I left. Then a friend from Colima did me the
favor of finding me housecleaning work—and I did that for
many years. The women I worked for at first recommended
me to others, and I stayed for a long time. From 1973 I stayed
here until 1982.

In 1982 I went back to Mexico. I was concerned about
my children and wanted to reestablish relations with them.
But they were angry with me, and so was my husband—so I
came back here to work.

Later my husband understood—through other people
who talked to him about how I lived here, how things were.
He wanted me to come back. And I returned and
reestablished my family ties. We lived there together and
then came here again and both worked for many years [until
1997, when they returned to Mexico].

So we have been together lately, but at the same time
separate. Recently [2001], for economic and other reasons,
he stayed in Mexico and I'm here working.

Now that I've had the opportunity to have some of the
things I never had as a child, I say, "It would have been better
to have them at fourteen or fifteen." Now I have a second pair
of shoes, a second dress. Then you had one dress—the one
you had on. To have a second dress was a big thing. I had to

make do for weekdays and Sundays with one pair of huaraches of the cheapest kind. Now, thank God, I have things—but it's not the same as having them when you are ashamed of what you wear. But anyway, I thank God that He allowed me to have a second pair of shoes. What else? That's it. And I don't know if it's good or what? Or should we go on?

Childhood and Adolescence

I remember there were a lot of problems when I was young. My mother suffered a lot with my father. He was very harsh with her, very offensive. He worked to drink. I remember that she worked very hard to provide for us and that my father worked and got drunk on the weekends. And he hit her a lot. I didn't know why or anything, just that he hit her a lot.

Sometimes we had to leave the house and sleep under a tree in a nearby pasture. The next day we would come back to the house and my father would be under control. And then it would happen again. It was the normal thing.

My father's brother came and took [her parents and her brother] to another town to live. I didn't want to go, and I stayed with my godmother of first communion. My mother got sick there, and my father came to get me—but I hid. Finally, he convinced me to go there to live with them. We were in Tamazula for a while and then returned to Tuxpan.

She died in Tuxpan. I'm not very sure. I must have been about nine.

That's when my tribulations started. My father hit me every weekend. He hit me. He would not let me go out—anywhere. I was just there in the house. And then there was the criticism from other people. I wondered, "Why do people hate me so much? Why don't people like me? What did I do to them?" As time went by, I realized that my mother cheated on my father with another man, and I thought, "That's why she suffered so much with him. He probably knew about it, and that was the cause of her suffering."

I couldn't keep a boyfriend. I realized that people were saying, "Like mother, like daughter." Mothers of boys who wanted to ask me to be their girlfriend quickly objected to me because of what people said—because of the bad example that my mother, may she rest in peace, left me. So I suffered.

My father would get drunk and bring friends to the house, and people started to say that they didn't come to drink, but only for me—that they were interested in me, that's why they came to the house. I said to my father, "You know what? I don't want you to bring your friends here. If you keep bringing your friends here, then I'm going to leave." He got annoyed and said, "Well, if you don't like it, you can leave. You know where the door is."

That's what happened. I let some time pass and it was the same, always the same. So, I decided to leave.

Victoria's father and her son's son on the farm near Tuxpan (1986).

I said to my brother, "Will you go with me?" He said, "If you're going to go, I'll go too."

I stayed with my godmother. She lived alone. She treated me okay, but she didn't let me go out at all. I never had a boyfriend. So I went to my aunt's. She had daughters, and I wanted to have girls around. I stayed there—always with the fear that people would criticize me because they knew about my mother. And that's how it was.

I knew one boy, but the same thing happened with his mother. She wouldn't let him go with me because who knew what would happen, what luck he would have, etc., etc., etc. I left him.

Marriage

Then I met the one who is my husband—after a lot of boyfriends who talked to me for two or three days or a week. He talked about marriage. I had a problem with him too, because his mother raised the same questions about my mother and who knows what else. That's how we started.

First he asked for my hand. The priest came to my aunt's house, but my aunt said that she couldn't decide—that my father should be the one to decide. So I contacted my father, who was living in another town, and he told me the date of his next visit to Tuxpan. When the priest came to him, he agreed, but said we should wait for three or four months—to make sure we did not want to back out.

In the living room of a relative's house where Victoria lived in 2001.

During that time I went to a fiesta and danced with someone who approached me; my boyfriend got mad, and we broke up for three months. He came and apologized. We made up, and he wanted me to go off with him, but I said, "No." He got drunk and threatened to come into the house and take me away. I was afraid he might do it and my aunt would have a problem with him, so I went. That was in March, and we got married on the tenth of May.

I went with him and, well, it was the same. I thought I was going to have a good life, but it didn't come out that way. He didn't trust me. He was very jealous, maybe because of what his mother told him. I couldn't go out anywhere. I couldn't raise my eyes because he thought that people were signaling me, that I was flirting. And that's how it was, years and years and years of this martyrdom.

I had my children. We made a very good friend of mine the godmother of our daughter. But there was a problem, because, according to her, she was in love with my husband. Because of the friendship and the godparent relationship we continued to see her.

First Period in the United States

The two of us came together, and I crossed before he did. He came and lasted three or four months, and the immigration caught him and threw him out.

I stayed here. I hadn't paid off the money that the lady where I worked had lent me to pay for crossing. I borrowed more money to pay for his crossing. So, when they threw him out, he was in Tijuana being pitied or whatever. He talked with me about it, but then, where I worked, they didn't tell me that he had called, and he thought that I wanted no part of him. So he got angry that he could not communicate with me. He got angry and he went back to Tuxpan.

Later he sent me a letter telling me that he was in Tuxpan and that I should not try to return there because, God knows how I was living here, what I was doing, because he couldn't communicate with me—and surely, I wanted no part of him. And it wasn't like that. I didn't know that he was calling me. And when he sent the letter, I couldn't go back because I owed the money. I owed what they charged for him, and I hadn't yet finished paying off what they charged for me. At this time I earned forty dollars a week.

FC: *What year was this?*
I entered at 5:00 p.m. on the fifth of January of 1973. We came from Tuxpan to Tijuana in 1972 and entered here in 1973.

FC: *How did you find work?*
Through my comadre. That comadre had been here for a while. She came to Tuxpan in December [1971] and she talked to us about coming. We came to Tijuana the next October.

The lady where I was going to work and the lady where my comadre worked were friends. The lady I was going to work for loaned me the money to pay for crossing. In those days there weren't many people working here.

Walking from the bus stop to her Saturday job.

I got the job quickly. I lasted at that job for three months. Then the lady had economic problems, and she had to leave, but she got me a job with a friend of hers. That's when I went to Laguna Beach, because I arrived to Corona del Mar. There opposite Fashion Island. The lady lived there. And from there I went to Laguna—to work there with another lady. She had three children. It was live-in too. Then I went to Los Angeles and took care of children—for relatives.

When I came back here, I got housecleaning day jobs—one with the woman where I went today. She has kept me with her. She has been very good. Very good because she is concerned about other people and not concerned about herself. She is a very good person. And with her and jobs that she got me with her friends, I had a full week. I've been working for her for twenty-some years.

Reconciliation with Her Husband

When my husband got angry and went back to Mexico, he said the worst about me to my children. My children got mad at me. I had completely lost my family, my home. It was lost for the ten years that I was here. Then I got my courage together and went to Mexico to confront him and my children. I went with my brother as my witness, because he always knew where I went. He knew about my life here.

In December 1982 Victoria arrived in Tuxpan with her brother and his family. She had not communicated with her husband and children for ten years—except for sending money orders for the family to her father, who lived with her husband and children on a farm outside of town. She arrived with many gifts and the stubs from all the money orders as proof of her continued attention to them.

Word that we were in Tuxpan spread. My daughter came to see me first—cautiously, and she would not accept any of the gifts. Then my son came. He wouldn't accept gifts either but said he would take them if we came to the farm.

My brother went to the farm with me. My husband had no problem with him. He talked to my husband and asked him to accept the gifts. My husband refused and said that the children did not need them, that we should take them away. Then he said to me, "If you are looking to get back together with me, forget it. I would not get caught dead with you." So we went back to Tuxpan and then back here.

They grew up without a mother. When I went there and brought the gifts, according to them I was trying to buy them with things. But despite everything, I never stopped helping them. I always sent them a little money. What little I earned I divided, part for my expenses and part to send to them. For them this was not enough. They wanted affection, and my boy was a little resentful. When he was in school and they wanted his mother, his father to go to a meeting, he didn't have anyone to go, and he was ashamed. I think that is why he left school. He left school and did not want to study anymore. For this reason he is still resentful, still ashamed. I'm not sure what is going on with him, but I understand because in that situation probably even I would do the same.

The children phoned her and wrote to her from Mexico. Her son came to the United States the next year with her help. He worked here for two years before going to Mexico to get married in 1985.

My son invited me to his wedding and I went. That's when my husband tried to get together with me again. "You know," he said, "I don't want you to go. Forgive me; notice that I'm not like I was before. I'm going to change. I've stopped drinking. I won't hit you anymore. I won't be jealous. It will be really different."

But I had my doubts. I said I would think about it. So I came back here, and he sent me letters and letters and letters—telling me not to be afraid, that he would be different. I talked with my brother and asked his advice. He said that it was my decision, that if I decided to go, he would support me, that if it didn't work out, I could call him and he would help me get back here. So, well, I decided to return to Mexico.

Her Comadre

When I decided to go back, I was living with my comadre who had helped us come here. I told her that I would no longer be helping her pay the rent, that I would not be coming back because I was going to try to go back to my husband, to reestablish my family.

"Haven't you noticed that I'm in love with you?" she said. "You in love with me?" I said, because I was surprised. We were friends from infancy, from childhood. From adolescence we had been in different situations. She had other friends. And after not seeing each other, we got together again and the friendship continued, because we became comadres. Why was she telling me this?

"You're not going to go," she said. "You're going to stay here with me. Why do you think I brought you here?" "No way," I told her. "I'm going. To me what's important is my children and my family," I said. "If you go, I'll kill you," she said. "One or the other . . . I'll kill you, or I'll kill myself. And it will be your fault."

So, I was surprised. I talked with my brother, and I told him all this. "Don't worry," he said. "I'll try to buy a ticket, and we'll try to get at least some of your things out. When she goes to work, we'll go in my pickup and get what we can, and we'll take them to the airport, and you'll go." That's what we did.

She wouldn't leave me alone after I said I was leaving. She took me to work and picked me up from work. One day when she dropped me off, I pretended to walk toward my job, and when I was sure that she had left, I doubled back and met my brother on a nearby street. She went to my jobs to ask where I had gone and to my brother's house in Los Angeles. But he was not there. He was at the airport.

It was shameful for me for her to go around saying that she was in love with me—that she loved me with all her soul, all her heart, with who knows what. I didn't know any of this until later when people told me everything that she had said. She said she was going to go to Tuxpan to look for me and that she was going to do things to me and my husband. We were afraid that she might do it, because we knew she had a pistol—that she had supposedly bought to do this.

But nothing happened. I went to Tuxpan, and there was no problem. And I learned that she had been there too, but she didn't do anything.

To the United States with Her Husband

When they began with the amnesty of the cards [based on IRCA, the Immigration Reform and Control Act, passed in 1986], I was in Mexico, and the ladies [employers] told me to come because, given all the time I had spent here, I might be able to get papers. They helped me. They gave me letters. And I was lucky. I got papers.

When I came, I brought my husband with me. He worked in Gonzales [near Salinas in northern California] on broccoli, and lettuce, and other vegetables, then picking lemons near Los Angeles, and then near South Coast Plaza [in Orange County] for a lady harvesting corn on the cob, lettuce, and onions. But the work slowed down. He worked only two or three hours per day.

I said, "If you want to, it might be better if you come with me. I will ask the ladies to see what they say." At this time I had a lot of work. I did two or three houses per day. We worked together in Corona del Mar, in Laguna Beach. We worked together—for about four years—until we left [in late 1997].

I didn't leave because I wanted to. My husband said that I was very tired. Because it was a lot of work.

In 2002 Victoria described her illness in greater detail. She said that when she and her husband left for Mexico, they thought the illness was due to the cleaning liquids used in her work here. Two years of treatment by various doctors in Mexico did not make her well. She woke in the middle of the night feeling that she would choke or suffocate and as a consequence was not able to sleep well.

They found a curer (curandero) in a distant town. He diagnosed her and recommended nine weeks of treatment that included rubbing an egg over her body in the problem areas, breaking it open, and reading the contents. The first week it had small grains or particles in it. So too the second and third weeks. On the fourth week the egg was clearer and she felt much better. She finished the recommended course of treatment. Victoria felt that the illness was sent by her comadre. She said that the curer did not want to name a specific person, but that signs he gave convinced her that it was her comadre.

Her Most Recent Trip

In late 1997 Victoria and her husband settled in Mexico. In March 2001 Victoria returned to the United States alone. Her husband, who is seventy, stayed alone on their land, where he raised chickens and pigs.

My card was running out, so I came to renew it. I was going to go back to Mexico, and I said to my husband that I might stay or come home, and he said, "Well, if you find a job, stay. If not, come back." I came to do an errand, but I stayed.

The day after I arrived, my son took me to the lawyer.

Going home after work.

In April 2002, a few weeks before her sixtieth birthday, Victoria said she felt she might be able to work here another two or three years.

She made out my papers and we took them, with the photos, to immigration. They didn't ask me any questions. They just looked at my old card and the other papers I brought. We left them there and went home. Later they sent a letter saying they had received the check. At the time we left the papers, they told me that it would take a year to get the new card, but it came in August—in four months.

When I arrived, I stayed with my son. I was there for a month or two, but I had to leave because the apartment is a little small, and they are five. So I had to look for a place.

I was renting a room in Santa Ana, but they didn't want me to keep the room so I went looking and I didn't find anything. So this girl [her cousin's daughter] said, "Come here. You can stay with me." That's why I'm here [in August 2001]. I'm her comadre too, but she calls me "aunt" out of respect.

In August 2001 Victoria had already found seven days of work for every two-week period. She also worked on her "niece's" jobs on Mondays and took every other Tuesday off. By April 2002 she had a full six-day schedule of her own— four houses that she cleaned every week and four that she did every other week.

When I got here, I talked with the lady [in Laguna Beach]. I was in Mexico for four years, and I left a niece with her. And she let my niece go to give me work when I came back. I told her to get me work with her friends and to keep my niece. And she didn't want to. "No," she said, "I've been waiting for you. Your niece was here because you left her— taking care of your job." So I'm with her again. I told my niece to keep the other jobs I had left her. I couldn't refuse this lady because she had helped me a lot. When I was in Mexico, she gathered contributions from her friends and sent me money. I told my niece, "I'm very sorry. I have to go to work with the lady because she has helped me a lot and I don't want to say no to her. She might think that I don't want to work for her or something." And I have kept working for her. She is a very good lady.

As I told you, if it weren't for her, I wouldn't have gotten my jobs as quickly. And as I said, she has always been attentive to me. Others might have said, "Now she's gone." She wrote to me and wrote to me, because she speaks a little Spanish. She would write to me and send me pictures of her family. When I was gone, she never stopped writing to me. I'll keep working for her as long as I can. I say that because one gets older, and things are not the same.

Sharon Risley lives and works in Laguna Beach. She provided this list of significant dates in her adult life:

1964 She graduated from high school and got married to her first husband.

1964 Her daughter Angela was born (October 11).

1968 She and Art (who became her second husband) moved into the house where she now lives.

1969 Her daughter Naomi was born (November 17).

1975 She and Art were married (February 14).

1976 Her son, Sol, was born (July 24).

1986 She and Art separated.

1989 She and Art divorced (late in the year).

1990 She received her BFA degree from the Art Institute of Southern California.

Sharon Risley

Okay. Well, I was born in Laguna in 1947, grew up on the beach, pretty much. My mother worked in town. My father worked in town. So it was a really pleasant childhood—very small town at the time. Even when I was in my early teens, I remember, Laguna Beach had, oh, not quite four thousand people. And in the wintertime the seagulls would come up and hang out on the street where the shops were, downtown. And a lot of shops closed in the winter. So it was a really, really nice place to grow up.

Then in my high school years my life changed a lot—a lot. So much happened in such a small amount of time that it's hard to even get into that part right now. Really. But needless to say, I ended up getting pregnant and getting married and graduating, no, getting pregnant, graduating, and getting married, all in about a month's time. I had applied for a scholarship to Chouinard Art Academy but lost it because I was pregnant. So my life did a real lot of changing in a very short period of time. I thought I was so grown up at sixteen. I look back now, at age fifty-four, and am just amazed at what I thought.

So I moved shortly thereafter to Connecticut and lived with my first husband and our daughter—for about a year and a half. And that was just really bad. He was an alcoholic, and it didn't work. I came back to California by myself with my daughter. Lived with my parents for a little while. By this time my parents' situation was very dysfunctional. And that's why I had left earlier. So, I didn't stay there too long. I ended up moving to Newport, back to Laguna, working where I could—doing waitressing.

In the meantime my ex-husband, who was in Connecticut, charged me with abandonment and legally took my daughter. So . . . you can do that in Connecticut. I left, because we agreed to separate, but anyway.

So then my life took a turn, quite a turn. I ended up living in San Francisco. It was about 1966 to about 1967. So I went through not quite two years—a whole lot of traveling and being a hippie, I guess. I met a lot of really interesting people, but I realized that was not where I wanted to put myself in life.

So I moved back to Laguna and met my second husband and proceeded to settle in this house and raise three kids—two of which were mine and one of which was his son, my stepson.

During that time my mother died. She was taking too many pills and then my dad started taking pills. And they were just a mess. Really a mess. Naomi was about a year old, and a policeman comes to the door to inform me that my mother has passed away, that she took an overdose of sleeping pills. She went to Las Vegas and took an overdose of sleeping pills. And died.

I lived here for about twenty years with Art. Then we had a family crisis and our marriage ended. It was this big explosion. At the time Naomi was sixteen, Sol was ten, Josh was eighteen, had just graduated from high school and was talking about moving up north and going to school. So, that was another real severe change in my life.

Sol continued to live with me. Naomi got married at age eighteen and had three children with her husband. My son, Sol, was a teenager that went through hell—almost lost him. And about age nineteen, he moved up north. And he's been doing okay. And Naomi has since left her first husband with three kids and is with a new boyfriend, and they have a child who's six. My first daughter, Angela, who continued to be raised in Connecticut, is moving back here, probably at the end of August.

And my son, Sol, who has learned how to manage his life, I hope, is coming back here to live with me in October—to help me fix up this house. Needs painting inside and out—numerous projects of repair, which I can't do anymore.

I used to do everything. Now I have limitations for the first time in my life—my hands, and I just can't go where I used to go. And so, I don't know if I'm going to stay here or what. But I want to put a small house on my garden property and either sell this house, or rent it out. And then make my decision after that whether I'm going to stay here.

But now, all my family's going to be back here. This would be a first. So, this will be different. I do not know how it's going to go. I feel like there has been a lot of dispersion—a lot of dispersion—throughout my life in different circumstances—but for some reason it seems like there's going to be a whole different kind of—I don't even know what to call it yet—kind of a gathering, for me and family.

End of story, I don't know.

That wasn't even ten minutes. Now, see, there's different parts of that I could elaborate on, but I didn't know; I kind of just did an outline.

FC: *Great. It was a great outline.*
Okay.

FC: *Is there any part you would want to elaborate?*
Yeah, which part would we want to elaborate? Gosh. I don't know.

Sharon did four elaborations. The first two are labeled for periods: teenage years and childhood, the last two for topics: family and work.

At work, "herding" the cat off the living room rug.

Teenage Years

Okay. Let's say I started working when I was about twelve years old. I mean having a job—a real job—away from home. It was working for the dentist who worked on my teeth—because I've always had problems with my teeth. So, I started going to a dentist early on—age four—Dr. Ott, who was an old-time dentist in town. And he refused to work on me because I would put up such a fuss about having my teeth drilled. So, he refused to work on me, and about that time, his son-in-law, Dr. Adler, was working in the same office. And so Dr. Adler started working on my teeth. And so through the years, that's the dentist I went to.

When I was about age twelve, Dr. Adler asked if I wanted to come in and clean the office on Saturdays—and said that if I would come on Tuesday and Thursday, I could learn with the dental assistant how to develop the x-rays, sterilize the instruments, mix the silver, et cetera. He said, "If you work with me through high school, you can have a job. You know, you won't have to go to dental hygiene school." I mean, this was back in the late fifties, early sixties. Okay. So I thought, This is good.

This was before I went off the deep end as a middle-aged teenager. So, at age twelve I was still pretty focused. So, I started working in the office. Every Saturday, I cleaned. Tuesdays and Thursdays, I'd come to help assist and learned a lot. It was very interesting. I felt very grown up, you know, at age twelve, having this kind of job. I was also taking dancing lessons and piano lessons. So my life was really full, you know. And I was enjoying it.

My parents weren't getting along too well at the time, and they shortly thereafter went through a series of being divorced, getting back together, not a complete divorce, and then separating. So we moved a little bit. Actually that was before I was ten. So, by the time I was twelve, we were back in Laguna.

And then I hit age thirteen, and my whole focus changed. It became dating and going out. I didn't party a lot—but just going out. And I still worked, but I wasn't taking the piano. I wasn't taking the dancing. I was in high school [*laugh*]. And my life became very unfocused. But thank God for a couple of art teachers in high school, Charlotte Ilgner and Miss Kapanki, because if it wasn't for them, I probably wouldn't have stayed focused at all, probably would have gotten in way more trouble. I actually ended up graduating, because I stayed in school for my art classes.

Childhood

Gosh, I guess I could have started with growing up in Bluebird Canyon—because that was really a highlight of my childhood. Bluebird Canyon is like this canyon. It's a couple of hills over. And at the time there was "old" Bluebird Canyon, but there wasn't anything like you see with the hills covered with houses the way they are now.

So, ah, early experience growing up in Bluebird Canyon was great. I mean, it was a place that you could play in the hills—of course my mother would freak out.

Sharon in her front yard. She lives in a community of forty-seven houses set on small lots that are separated by narrow lanes and lots of plants. Parking spaces are in areas at the edge of the community. Many of the people who live there are artists. She is active in community projects.

Sharon in her living room with a map of the community and adjoining subdivisions that she made for a project in the early 1980s.

I'd go down the hill, across the street, and up on the next hill, and there was a corral over there that had, like, a burro. I thought it was a donkey, but it was probably a burro. And I used to get on that fence and wait until I could get on the back of that burro—to see if I could ride him. Okay. And I used to go over there all the time. I don't think my mother realized it. I used to go far and wide. I liked to explore.

My dad's mother—well, I'd say it was his adopted mother, Nana—lived in Las Vegas, and she would always send these pinafore dresses, really nice dresses, to my mom for me or to me. Okay. My mom would dress me up in these dresses, and I'd go out, play exploring, and go across the street to try and ride the burro, and I'd come home so incredibly askew and a mess that she would just freak out. I didn't want to tell her where I was playing, so I'd say I fell or whatever. I was making a fort in the hillside. I was a tomboy. I really was. I mean, I liked the dresses, but really it was more fun to go explore and play.

I remember playing in the hillsides, tall weeds, getting lost. You know, at the time it scared me. I thought, My God, I don't know how to get back home. Right? But I look back on that now, and I savor that. I totally savor it. Being able to explore like that as a kid.

And when I raised my kids here, I think I was trying to give them some of what I experienced when I grew up in Bluebird Canyon. And they got it. They were able to play here. They had a whole hillside they could play on—an area that wasn't just in the street, in the town, whatever. But for them to raise their kids here is not so easy.

Family

Okay. Let's see. About the time I was sixteen, I had a boyfriend. Actually I had a boyfriend from the time I was fourteen. He was twenty, going on twenty-one. We were afraid to tell my parents that he was that old. So we lied. But this was a really interesting fellow, and he became very close with my parents and me. And we had even thought about getting married, but never went there.

My mom, at this point, she was pretty much in a state of depression—and didn't work anymore and stayed home a lot and took a lot of pills that the doctors prescribed for her, actually way more than she needed, but, you know, it was the age of Librium and birth control pills to regulate you and combinations of pills that I really think were very bad for her.

And I remember one night Bob [Sharon's boyfriend] and I were talking, and he just laid out to me the fact that my mother had never told me—that my father was not my real father. And I took it in. I listened. The reason my mother had never told me is because she had madea pact with my dad, the father that raised me, to never divulge this information. So, I took it in stride and Inever said a word about it. I just put it in the back of my head.

And you know, I had feeling when I was a kid there was something different about me. But I know every kid will go through that. But I do believe that there were things unsaid that I could feel as a child, and that's why I came up with that category of being different.

The lane as it passes Sharon's house.

When it all came out, my mom said, "Who'd you find out from?" My dad said, "Who did you tell?" It was just this big scene, but nothing really got resolved. And nothing still really got said. The dust settled. So my life just went on. I ended up getting married and graduated from high school and went to Connecticut.

Now this one's going to hook me, okay? I'm an emotional person, I'm sorry. None of this stuff hit me until I was about thirty-one, and I had my son. All of a sudden I started thinking about who my biological father was, and where was my mother. And then about age forty-two, my whole family fell apart here.

Now, another twelve years later, I don't have much immediate family. I guess that's why my interest in genealogy. I know that I have an uncle, my mother's brother, that I would like to find. He'd be seventy-six if he's still alive. He just like disappeared in 1962.

The other person that I'd like to find is my biological father. Through the years I've gathered little bits of information because no one's ever really either known or wanted to talk about it—or they spent so many years not talking about it that they don't remember. My dad has said to me before—see, there's this whole small town thing. My mother worked in town at age fourteen, fifteen, and sixteen. Her two uncles owned a restaurant or two restaurants in town in the late thirties. She worked for one of them. Maybe it was about 1946.

My dad should tell me, but I just feel like I should be sensitive. So I said, "Dad! You gave Mom money for a divorce, then she must have been married!" And so I just said it. I said, "Dad, how do we know that that isn't my father?" I just came out and said it. He says, "Well, we don't." He says, "Only your mom does." So that's kind of where that's been left at, okay.

But what I did do was I got on the Internet and I wrote to the Health and Vital Statistics Department of San Diego County and inquired about how I go about finding out who my mother married in 1945, late '45 to '46, I believe—it was a short period of time, with just her name and not her spouse's name. So I'm tracking it that way.

I don't know why I got off on this tangent, but it's a big part of my life at this point. Period.

Work

FC: *One thing I'm interested in is the work, what I call the work history.*
Okay, I'll give you a short history of my work thing.

FC: *You started when you were twelve, and then…*
Cleaning venetian blinds in the office. The thing I hated the most. And it was an office with lots of windows. All covered with venetian blinds. And I hated it. Sometimes when I really want to put myself in a corner and beat myself up, I go, "My God, Sharon, you're fifty-four; you're still doing the same thing."

With friends who live on the same lane.

Spreading straw on the garden property where she hopes to build a house. It is just down the lane from her present house.

I know better than to go there, but sometimes I get a little depressed. I'm really talented. I feel sometimes that I've never found my niche. Then I go, "It's on you, Sharon. When have you ever really focused on one thing at a time?" I focus on twenty things at once. So maybe it's part of that.

I didn't go back into housecleaning away from home until I got divorced from my husband of twenty years. At the time, I was two years into school at what is now called the Art Institute of Southern California. I'd gotten a scholarship, a series of scholarships and grants to go to school. Then I decided, "I really like this." So I applied for student aid and decided to go ahead and do a four-year thing.

The family crisis started in 1986, when I was in the middle of school. I still had Sol and was not getting any help from my ex-husband, and court took like three years. He was fighting me for the house and fighting me for custody of Sol. I'm still a little bitter about it. It was really grueling and ugly and horrible, the whole thing. And the fact that he would fight me in court, it just really topped it off.

I don't talk to him and haven't for years. I just don't. He doesn't communicate with the kids. It's like he's not a part of their lives, and this is very hurtful. Hurtful for so many different reasons, you know. And I had to really back off from that one and realized that this is still my kids' father and his relationship with them is his relationship with them and theirs with him. It has nothing to do with me.

In 2002 Sol returned to Laguna Beach, lived with his mother part of the time, and got in touch with his father.

Collecting snails under the fig tree on her garden property.

I had to really just back off from that whole thing and leave it up to God. I didn't mean to cry so much. And I went back to the family thing and went away from the work.

FC: *That's what you care about, instead of work. It's pretty clear.* Well, you know, the work thing is what, thank God, has kept me able to forge ahead and do what I want to do. And I'm immensely grateful for that, because during the time when my son was still trying to survive being a teenager and the whole dysfunctionalness of the situation, I could be available at any time. I could manipulate my schedule for work. I could pick my days. I could still go to school. I could still go to court. So really, I have to say that the kind of work, it's like self-employed contract labor, has afforded me the freedom to survive in a funny kind of way, even though it's the same work I was doing since I was twelve.

That's not the whole part of it. That's just on a personal level with myself kind of kicking my butt, going, "Why didn't you develop other skills?" Early on through the twenty years that I lived here, my ex-husband was an incredible artist, an incredible photographer, and I did get into making my jewelry and a lot of creative things, but I also was a total homebody, had a garden, had chickens and ducks, my fruit trees, you know. Everything was out of my house. Our shop was our house too, through the years. Before I added on the kitchen when I reroofed the house in '91, that whole area was the workshop—did casting, fabrication of lapidary. We had a very creative atmosphere and shared that part together, which was really nice.

I didn't really start cleaning houses until about '84. I started going back to work in '84. That's when I could see that Art and I were—things weren't right. I went back to work full-time then. I worked at the Sawdust Festival [a summer arts fair in Laguna Beach] in one of the food booths, juice stands, and I ended up running it.

I started doing housecleaning with a couple of other gals, part-time, and then in '86 I started working on my own because I needed more income when Art and I split up. So I've been doing it about fifteen years now, fourteen years. Solidly.

Before I started doing housecleaning full-time, I was working for other artists doing jewelry cleanup—people that I know that were sculptors, doing the cleanup on the waxes before it's cast, a lot of that kind of stuff. And then I continued to do that up until just recently, actually. So I don't know—I haven't just cleaned houses and worked for other artists. And I had gone to school too, actually, during all that time. When I'm doing stuff like that, it equals it out a little bit. I don't feel like I'm still cleaning venetian blinds.

I'm getting older. My hands are getting worn out is what's happening. I doubt I'll ever be able to really make jewelry again. I mean, I could do waxes, carving, but that was never my forte. I always did fabrication and liked doing it that way. I doubt I'll ever do that again. Clay, I could do that again. I just don't have it set up to do it. What I really want to get back into is drawing and painting. That would be so kind on my hands. No problem.

With her son, Sol, in November 2002.

Sharon at work.

I feel like I'm in a really big transition period in my life right now. I would like to phase the housecleaning down and up some of the other stuff. But I have such great people I work for now. It took a while to get here. It did. I was cleaning for real estate companies in between tenants and stuff like that. They want you to do ten years' worth of work and work miracles in eight hours sometimes.

But I don't do that anymore. In fact, I've had really good customers now for probably a good ten to twelve years solidly, Art and Carole being the oldest customer, dear friends, and then the others. . . . I've really had a different kind of clientele in the last ten years, which has been really great. I'm not dealing with some of that other baloney that you can get into. I really never wanted to get into hiring a crew. I just don't want to go there.

My dad's always saying, "Sharon, why don't you hire and train some girls?"

I don't want to do that. I never thought of this as being some kind of full-time occupation. Ever. Just something I always did know how to do, could do without thinking.

I really get into just kind of organizing things and getting into maintenance. Because it's what I had to do here—to run a tight ship with three kids. It didn't use to be this cluttered. Everything was all organized and built in. When I took the roof off, to redo the roof, I got rid of a lot of stuff that had been built in. We never had furniture. It was always built in. Really. Because this place was too small for furniture. The beds were built in. Seat area built in. Storage underneath, you know, stuff like that.

So, the customers I've had in the last ten years have been wonderful people to work for. I'm immensely grateful for that. And probably as I get older, there's a couple of customers that I can keep, but I don't really want to take on new jobs.

And I really and truly don't know how much longer I can seriously do the kind of work I do and maintain the quality of the kind of work I like to do in this field with these hands. They're getting crippled, and I'm in denial. I never had physical limitations. So I don't know what the future holds for me in this particular occupation, but it's served me very well through a total falling apart of my family and divorce and trying to raise kids and then having my daughter come back and live with me through her trials of being separated and having my grandkids live here. It's really afforded me the opportunity to stay and survive, and that's not been easy. Break!

In fall 2001, Esperanza Mejia lived with her son, Francisco Orellana, in an apartment about two blocks from her sister Leidi's apartment. Around that time her household changed in many ways. The year before, her daughter, Gabi, had finished high school and moved out. In fall 2001 her divorce from Francisco's father, Paco, became final, and she met Brad Guerre, whom she married at the end of the next year. During the period when she and Francisco were alone in the apartment, she needed help with the rent and briefly rented space to a couple and their small child.

Esperanza Mejia

Life in Guatemala

Well, to begin, I'll tell you that I have memories since I was seven. I remember that I had a very beautiful teacher when I was in the first grade. It was a very big school. All of us went, little boys and little girls.

And suddenly, we had to move, because my father changed his work. We moved to a very nice house—a house with two stories. I had to move to another school, to meet different children. And I remember that my father had to work very hard. But what he was earning was not enough to support the family, and my mother also had to work very hard. She made bread and sold everything she made. This was the way they supported us.

I was the baby of the family—of seven sisters and one brother. I was very pampered. We went to school and grew up. The government gave us everything free—because my father worked in a government company. We didn't pay anything. This lasted until the sixth grade. We were a very poor but a very united family.

Then we had to move to get to schools like junior high school. We went to another city. There I began what

would be the eighth grade. But I remember that my mother had many economic problems, because my father got sick.

My father died when I was seventeen. So then I moved to a big city because I had to work. I stopped studying. I worked in a store, and I loved my job. I was the cashier. It was a fabric store. I would have been happy even if they didn't pay me. I stayed in the job for six years.

To the United States

And then my sister [Leidi] decided to travel to the United States. She came illegally. It was a dangerous adventure. She had to travel in buses and trains and cars and to sleep in places with strange people. It took her two months to reach the United States. She said that it was very difficult here, and that life was very hard here—but that she liked it. Meanwhile others of the sisters were married.

I was very afraid of traveling. Let me say something else. My sister had invited me to come to the United States. I went to get a visa, and they gave it to me.

Francisco at his tae kwon do class.

But the problem was that I had a daughter. I had met someone who made many promises. I began to go out with him, and when he saw that I was pregnant, he left me. He said, "I'm going to Miami because I want a better future for you and the baby." But he never returned. I waited for him for four years. He came to visit me, but I could see that he didn't want responsibility for me or my daughter.

My sister came and said to me, "You have a daughter, and the situation is very difficult here, more difficult here than in the United States." She said, "I'll help you." But I thought about it too long. By the time I decided to travel, the visa was no longer valid. When I went to renew the visa, they told me that I'd had my opportunity, that I couldn't have another.

I decided to come illegally—and it was the most frightening trip of my life. But I wanted to get here. It took me a month and a half. And I traveled in many ways. First on buses for many days, on a train, in cars. We stayed in very poor parts of Mexico. In some there were not places to wash. They were small villages. Until one day, I think it was the seventeenth of January, 1986, I arrived.

Work as a Live-in Nanny/Housekeeper

At the beginning I was very depressed. I said to myself, "What am I doing here?"

I had left my daughter. She was just two and a half. And, thank God, I found a job caring for children.

At work.

That's how I began. But I was very depressed. I was with a family that was certainly very good. I couldn't complain. They helped me a lot. They were very nice to me. They spoke to me in Spanish, which was good, because I didn't speak any English.

But I wanted to earn more money, and I asked the woman if I could have a raise. And she said, "No, that's not possible. I'm paying you well." At that time she was paying me sixty dollars per week. I was talking with people who rode the bus with me, and they said, "This woman is exploiting you." They said, "It's not just"—because I was telling them everything I did. I was working from 5:30 a.m. until 5:00 p.m. and I was uncomfortable because the woman was telling me that at 5:00 p.m. I had to be in my room, because she did not want her husband to see me. I didn't know why. She said, "I want privacy with my husband." And I was living with them.

I finally decided to quit. I found a better job—with a family—a couple who were both lawyers. I was doing the same work—taking care of the children and doing all the housework. And one day—I thought I was doing a very good job—I asked the woman if they could help with my papers, to make me legal in this country. She said, "Yes, why not?"

But I had bad luck. I was changing one of the babies and it fell out of the crib. The woman became hysterical. I understood that it was my fault. But it was also an accident. She shouted at me in an ugly way, and it hurt me very much because I felt that for me, the children were very important, and besides taking very good care of the children, I kept the house very clean. I was doing everything. And they traveled a lot. They left me alone with the children for as long as two weeks. And when I had the accident, she shouted at me that I was irresponsible. It hurt me very much. I said, "Well, if you think I am irresponsible, why do you have me here in your house? It was an accident; it could have happened to you or to your husband." She said, "But my husband is not happy." "Fine," I said. "Then I'll look for another job, and thanks for everything."

I left the job with the lawyer. She was paying me $235 per week. For that period, it was very good pay, for she knew that the responsibility was very great. She had me working almost twenty-four hours a day. She made me responsible for the children at night—because the children slept very close to my bedroom. "When the baby cries," she said, "it wants to eat or to have its diaper changed." I wasn't sleeping so I could attend to the baby before the parents awoke. I was very stressed, very tired. I had adapted myself to it, but I didn't have a life. Day and night I was attending to the children and the house—as well as the animals that they had. It was a lot of fun [*with light sarcasm*], because she insisted that the children be taken care of well, that the animals be fed, and that I care for the rest of the house. So I left that job.

That's when I decided that I didn't want to take care of children—that I just wanted to clean houses. I'd had two experiences, and that was enough.

I had been working for them [the lawyers] for two
years. Fortunately, the woman had given me an excellent
letter to immigration, and with that letter I got my
green card. That was about two and a half years after
I arrived here.

When I could, when I received my green card, the
first thing I did was to go to Guatemala to see my daughter.
At that time my daughter was four and a half, almost five.
It was a wonderful thing. I don't know if I deserved it, but
it was a gift that God gave me. By that time I had adapted
to this country—but my mother, my daughter, and the rest
of my family were in Guatemala. I thought, Should I stay
here [in Guatemala] or should I return to the United States,
going legally? I decided to return here. But I promised my
daughter that I would do every thing possible to bring her
to the United States legally. Which I did, thank God, in less
than three years.

Housecleaning, School, Husband, and Children

It's hard to begin cleaning houses. I began with one. It
took me years to fill the week—one house for each day.

I decided I had to go to school. I wanted to learn
English. And I began going to school after work. At that
time I didn't drive. I did it all by bus. It seemed like I spent
all my time traveling. Home to work, work to home—
arriving quickly to eat, bathe quickly, and go to school.

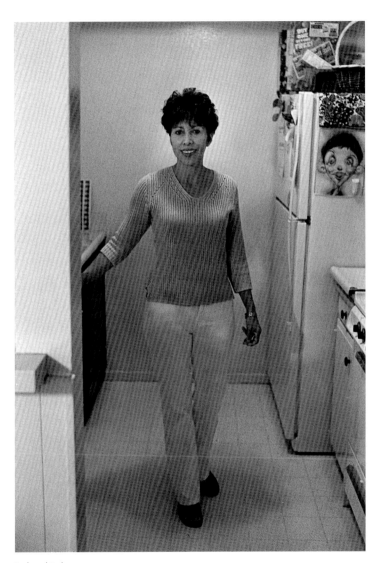

In her kitchen.

It was a very busy life. I think I learned a lot during those years in school.

Later, in the school, I met my husband. I never imagined that I would meet someone from my country. For sure, at first he didn't appeal to me. I didn't like it that he called me *"paesanita"* [little countrywoman]. It really irritated me that he did that. But I grew to like him more and more, and after a year we talked, not of marriage, but of living together—after about a year of knowing each other. We decided that we wanted to live together. I liked how he did things—that he wanted to learn English. I knew that he worked, that he was very responsible. He was a bachelor. He hadn't been married. He didn't have children. So I said, great, this is a man for me.

I really wanted to have another child. But the problem was that I wanted to have my daughter with me, and I said to him, "I don't want to have more children until I have my daughter with me." And, thank God, I succeeded in doing it.

When my daughter arrived, I wanted to avoid getting pregnant—because I wanted to enjoy her. I hadn't had her for many years. I had left her for six years.

Lamentably, or I'm not sure whether it was lamentable or fortunate, but this very year I got pregnant. And it happened that my daughter was very, very jealous. So, instead of uniting, we separated. I felt I was losing my daughter every day, every day. She was jealous, not only of my pregnancy, but because I had a man who was not her father. I felt that she felt a tremendous repulsion for my husband. And I said, "Why? He's very nice with you, he tries to make you happy." He took us out to entertaining places on the weekends—to make her happy. But he never made her happy.

Soon my son was born. She felt a horrible jealousy. I felt that she approached my son, but that sometimes it was like a repulsion that she felt, "Why, now that I have arrived, he arrived too, and he is going to take away what I could have had?" So, she grew up with this jealousy. I started to think that if my husband was not around, we would be happy. And I thought of leaving him to see if we would get closer. But that didn't happen.

I think, because of the jealousy with my son, and because she did not have my company, she began to rebel. She was very rebellious. I was called from the school because she was skipping out. She falsified my signature. When she was almost thirteen, she began to have a boyfriend. That seemed to me very premature—at her age. And she wanted to leave the house. She didn't come home to sleep. For me it was a great anguish; I didn't know what to do. I thought, If I'm sweet with her, she'll take advantage of it; if I'm tough, it's worse, because she'll flee. I never abused her. I never abused her, not physically nor verbally. I cried a lot. She was always telling me, "You never did anything for me. You abandoned me."

At her daughter, Gabi's, high school graduation. Their group left to right: her sister Leidi with Monica in front, Esperanza with Francisco in front, Gabi, Gabi's friend.

And I think that all this affected my relation with my husband. It had a big effect. I was always nervous, stressed. There was not harmony in my home.

Nevertheless, I wanted to improve myself—I thought of going to school, perhaps forgetting my problems a bit, and I decided I wanted to be a medical assistant. I started to go when my son was two, or perhaps one and a half. I started

going to school without stopping my work. I worked from 8:30 a.m. to 4:00 p.m. By then I was driving. Transportation was easier. The medical assistant course lasted almost a year and a half. It was very, very difficult. Many times I decided to stop, because it was too hard for me. Not only because of the language, but also because of being tired and stressed— the problems. But there was always someone who said,

"No, you have to finish. You started. Finish. You will succeed." Thank God, I listened to those people.

I think my English is not too bad. Nor is it very good. It's between 60 and 70 percent. And I had a friend from El Salvador. When we didn't understand the class, we taped it. My friend was married to an American, and he helped us a lot. He helped us with translation. We took the tapes to her house and he entered it on the computer and gave us the pages so that we could study them.

I felt that there was a lot of discrimination in the class. My friend and I were the only Hispanics. They looked at us as if they thought, What are they doing here? Don't they understand? But my friend said, "No, we have to continue." We supported each other. Well, the final exam arrived. You probably won't believe me. The two of us got the highest grades on the final exam. I was so happy. There were even people who didn't pass the test. I was so proud of myself. I finished. I finished my schooling. I was also proud because I wanted to show my daughter that I could do it.

To a certain point, I felt that this made her even more jealous of me. She seemed more separate from me. She behaved worse. Once, while I was studying for a final exam—here at this table—she was pacing back and forth so much that I was getting seasick. I said, "Do you want to tell me something?" "Yes," she said. "Okay, tell me." "Well, my boyfriend and I are having sexual relations." For me, it was like, "Oh, my God." "You're kidding," I said. "No," she said. "I wanted to tell you before someone else told you." "Oh, well," I said. "I won't do anything to you. Thanks for telling me directly. But this doesn't make me happy. It makes me very sad, because I brought you to this country with many dreams—so you could have a better future— better than mine. You can't combine two things—study with sex. You can do one thing or the other. So you have started. You won't stop—because, it's bad to say, but starting sex is like starting drugs. It's an addiction."

Well. That night I couldn't sleep. I spent it crying. She was almost a little girl. She was sixteen. It's a shame. "Why? I haven't set a bad example for you. While you have been here with me, I have been in only one relation- ship. I have not set a bad example for you. Tell me something," I said. "Has my husband abused you in any way? Is this why you are unhappy? Is this why you are so defensive—as if you are going to be attacked?" I said to her, "It's not just. Why are you doing this to me now that I need to be tranquil, to concentrate, to relax?" She said, "I'm not doing it to hurt you." Well, that passed. Thank God, she finished school.

Her mother in Guatemala (1998).

Her Mother and the Doctors

I worked as a volunteer medical assistant for a long time—because I wanted to get experience, because you finish school, but you don't really learn until you are doing the work. Right? And I noticed that I wasn't going to make a lot of money in this career. But I liked getting the practice. Because, I said, if someday I want to leave my housekeeper work, I'll be ready for another career. And I was also happy to learn what I learned, because I applied it a lot when my mother got sick.

That was two years ago, when she was in this country. I noticed that the symptoms she had were those of ministrokes. They began with loss of memory. She couldn't coordinate her ideas. She stopped talking. We took her to the doctor, but since she was a visitor in the United States, the doctor said, "No, your mother is very well; she doesn't have any problems. Take her home." This hurt me a lot, because she was a visitor but was still a human being.

I told the doctor, "What you are doing is unjust. My mother is having ministrokes." He said, "I'm sorry. I'm the doctor here." "I realize that," I said, "but I know what is going on." They had my mother in observation for three days, and he said, "That's enough. Take her with you. Your mother is well. She is faking because she wants the attention of her children." I said to him, "That's a lie. My mother has all the necessary attention of her children." I remember that it was winter. It was raining hard. That's when he told me that she was well. I said to him, "If this lady were your mother, would you take her out of the hospital? I don't think so."

The next day I traveled with her to Guatemala. When we arrived in Guatemala, the doctor told me, "There's nothing that can be done. It's very sad, but it's likely that your mother has two months or three months of life left." And it got worse and worse. Until the end arrived. She died three months after I took her there.

I think it was a great trauma for me. For that moment on, I said, "I don't want to help doctors. I don't want to work as a medical assistant." I left and kept working as a housekeeper—but not because I didn't feel capable of doing the job I studied for. I told my sister, "I don't want to work for stupid doctors who could have helped Mother and didn't do it." Honestly, I don't know what she died of, but while she was here, what she had was ministrokes. I don't know if they could have done anything for her.

When I returned here after my mother died, the bills from the hospital started to arrive. And they were for Mrs. Carmen de Mejia. It gave much great pleasure to say to the doctor, "I'm sorry, but the lady died. The lady you are looking for died, and I can give you a death certificate. Who's going to pay you? You said that she had nothing wrong with her. She died three months after you sent her away from the hospital." And I don't know, I think I was traumatized by seeing the bad practices of the doctors. While I was a volunteer medical assistant, I noticed how they treated people. They were doing unnecessary exams, and for people with insurance, they would list exams they didn't do. And they live off of this. I don't know. I was so disappointed that I decided I didn't want to do this work.

The housekeeper job was very hard work, but if I did it fast, I could spend more time with my son. It gave me a flexible schedule, and I earned more. I had the great luck of working for very nice people who have trusted me completely. And that's why I stayed at this work. The woman I work for is offering me the down payment for my house. They have given me many opportunities. And sometimes, it's not what you are given, but the way you are treated.

Divorce and Engagement

Esperanza and her husband, Paco (Francisco), were together for eleven years. Late in the period her husband began a relationship with another woman. They stayed together for some time but eventually divorced. Their son lives with her—except for weekends, when he is with his father.

This month [November 2001] I'm going to become single and free to begin a new life. I feel proud of myself because no matter how much wrong he did me, I have always tried to get along with him—for my son. I accept that he comes whenever he wants, that he goes out with my son.

A family portrait made in November 2001 at Esperanza's request. The women, left to right, are Esperanza; her daughter, Gabi; her niece, Monica; and her sister Leidi. The men, left to right, are Eduardo Juarez; Brad Guerre; her nephew, Gabriel Ramirez; and her son, Francisco. Eduardo and Gabi and Brad and Esperanza were married in 2002.

And I always tell my son, "Communicate with your father, call your father, tell him that you love him a lot, that you miss him." And thank God they have a very good relationship. "And above all," I tell him, "you have to respect your father a lot. He loves you very much."

And I thank Paco a lot too because, ever since the moment he left, he has always respected me. He has never tried to come back to me or abuse me verbally or anything. He also tells my son that he has to respect me a lot. We try to never say, "Oh, your father isn't correct," or, "Your mom's lying." We always try. And that's how the marriage ended.

In late summer 2001 Esperanza began dating a man whom she met when he came to do repairs at a house where she was working.

Now, the truth is that I don't know. Right at this moment I feel happy. I met a person that, for the first time in my life, has treated me like a woman, like a person. And it's marvelous, right? I told Paco—because this is recent— "Don't let it surprise you. At any moment when you arrive to visit your son, you may find a person that's interested in me, and I'm interested in him."

With her sisters Mirza, Leidi, and Yolanda at her wedding (2002).

December 28 (2002).

We've gotten along marvelously, and what I like most about him is that he's very religious. I think that a person that has knowledge about God respects God, respects his rules. And I barely started going out with him about a month and a half ago, and he's very nice. I love the way he treats me, the way he treats my son, and the respect with which he treats me above all because, it's ugly to say it, Frank, but nowadays men only look for sex.

It was something that surprised me so much. I tell him, "I don't want to think about the future. Maybe I'm not ready, but I love the present and that we live day by day." And every day we become closer, we identify more with each other. Because he comes here and he says, "I feel accepted, and I feel that I have a family." After a month of seeing each other, he took me to his house and introduced me to his mom, and now for Thanksgiving we're planning on going to where his sister lives. He wants me to meet his sister, and it's very nice.

I feel like . . . like I'm in the clouds. It's something very pretty, something I had never experienced. Like I tell you, I don't want to think about the future, but . . .

Mimi Lopez has four children. The twin girls, Julieta and Noemi, were born in Miami shortly after she arrived in the United States in 1985 and now live in Boston with her brother's family. She met her husband, Abel Orellana, in Southern California in 1992. In fall 2001 they lived with their children, Vivian and Abelito, in the same large apartment complex as Esperanza Mejia and her son, Francisco.

Mimi stopped cleaning houses a few months before her son was born in December 1999. Soon she and her husband found it hard to pay the nine-hundred-dollar rent on their one-bedroom Orange County apartment. Although Abel often worked more than forty hours per week and usually earned about nine dollars an hour, his earnings were not enough to sustain them and their two children.

In November 2001, when the rent had increased to $960, they temporarily moved in with relatives while Abel's brother completed the purchase of a four-bedroom house in a Riverside County city with less expensive housing. A few days before Christmas they moved there to share the house with him. Abel's brother, Paco (Francisco), is Esperanza Mejia's ex-husband.

Julieta Noemi (Mimi) Lopez

My name is Julieta Noemi Lopez [In family and work situations she identifies herslf as "Mimi"], and I am originally from El Progreso, Jutiapa, Guatemala, Central America, the daughter of Efrain Lopez and Refugio Flores Palmas. I am the fourth of seven children, and I remember that my childhood was very nice. My parents were always united. The best time was when we were in elementary school.

When I was fifteen or sixteen years old, they inaugurated the junior high school in my town. I completed only two grades there. After that, I didn't want to continue studying.

In 1977, when I was twenty-one, I had three siblings living in the capital, Guatemala City. I went there to live with my sister, who had already graduated as an accountant—and my entire family wanted me to continue studying. After I studied for a while in a secondary school, I decided to pursue a two-year course as a commercial secretary.

But I never liked the capital. I graduated and decided to return to my town. I liked my big house there—with my dad and, more than anything, with my mom. I've always been very close to my mom. We decided to start a business, a mini-supermarket that is still open. My parents and my siblings have been managing it.

In 1985 I came to Miami and worked taking care of a three-month-old baby. I was more like a mother to the baby because he slept with me in the room; I would spend the whole day with him.

But we lived together for a very short time because my two little girls were on the way. They were born premature, and after twenty days they were still very small. I felt a lot of responsibility, and I was alone in this country, so I decided to return to Guatemala. There I worked in the store, and as time went by, my little girls grew up.

About five years later our economic situation was getting worse every day, and a job came up in the United States. Thank God, I had my documents in order so that I could travel. One of my sisters was a friend of the sister of a lady that needed someone to work in Atlanta. I left my girls in Guatemala and came here to work—to provide for them.

I worked in Atlanta for two years as a live-in—two years without going to Guatemala. When the couple separated, I decided to return to Guatemala. I stayed there for three months, and from there I came to California. And I've been here in California nine years, since 1992.

Mimi's parents (about 1990).

At first I worked in houses as a live-in the whole week. On the weekend, well, I would go out. I stayed with some of my cousins—they would take me to work and pick me up on the weekends. Then another job came up. And I decided to change and go with another lady for whom I would babysit. I had a third job. Well, one's always looking to see where one gets paid more.

In the third job I was making two hundred dollars a week. I felt that was a lot of money. I was very happy because I could help my daughters and my family mostly by sending them money. This was the last job where I lived in. The gentleman was from Israel and the lady was American, very good people.

Then I got married, and slowly I began to have more and more houses to clean. Now I don't clean houses. I am taking a break from the routine—from getting up early to leave our kids.

Now I have two more children. Vivian is six and Abelito is twenty-two months old, and here we are taking care of them while they grow a little more.

We'll see if in the future God helps us find a job so that I can help my husband, because it's very difficult for the man to carry all the responsibilities in the home. Especially now that we are living in difficult times, with prices higher and higher every day.

So I think that I already arrived to the last memory of my life—from childhood until now. I'm forty-five years old. We'll see what our destiny has prepared for us in the future.

With Abelito and Vivian outside her Orange County apartment.

FC: *Let's see, then, if there are, I don't know, themes. Can you amplify a bit, I don't know on what part—how you met your husband, or how your children were born or, well, your little girls' life? Well, whatever you choose, right?*

Her Older Daughters, the Twins

Well, first we'll talk about my older daughters. I met their dad in Guatemala. He was a very jovial person; he was very attentive, very well mannered. I don't have bad memories about him because he died already. I remember that I was eighteen or twenty, more or less, when he used to visit my house a lot. I felt that he was too old for me. And then, I didn't want to take anyone seriously. I had always been afraid of having responsibilities, but he used to come by really often, and when he came by, I used to leave home and leave my mom in the little store. I would go to one of my aunts. And this is how slowly one, two, three, four years passed.

After about five years I saw him again and he started to always visit me, and visit me, and I believed in him. I trusted him, and that's how, by believing his promises, I allowed myself to be guided by what he told me. And that's how the two little girls were born—from a free union. I was never tied to him. When I found out that he really just wanted to play with my feelings, I separated from him, but without knowing that I was pregnant. Without knowing, because I remember that I had been with him only once. In those days, I decided to come to the United States.

I had always been, and I still am, a person that when I think someone is going to hurt my feelings, I try to distance myself from that person. I came running away from him because he had cheated me. He just wanted to play with my feelings, and I came and stayed here. After the girls were born, my family went and told him that two girls had been born. My daughters have only my last name.

The girls were famous. Someday they'll have the opportunity to go to Miami and look for some media so that they can remember or be interviewed about their birth—because they were born on Thanksgiving. And I didn't even have time to go to the hospital. I had the girls by myself. I cut their umbilical cords, and when the paramedics arrived, I had already wrapped them in blankets. We came out on the covers of all the newspapers in Miami—for having had them on my own and for them having been born on Thanksgiving.

Thank God the girls were born very healthy, and I thank God also for giving me my girls. I never rejected them. When I felt I was pregnant, I always told God, "Thank you, God! I'll always love my daughter." But I never thought there would be two of them.

And, thank God, my family never rejected them. They are still the most important ones in my family. They had a very good childhood, a very good upbringing. My entire family is Christian, and the girls, thank God, are following in the footsteps of what they were taught in their childhood. Now they are here in the United States, preparing themselves for what life has in store for them.

Local News

Saturday, November 30, 1985   The Miami Herald   Section B

Woman delivers her own twin girls

Scotch is used to sterilize scissors for birth in Cricket Club penthouse

MARY LOU FOY / Miami Herald Staff

Twin sisters Noemi, left, and Julieta asleep in their incubators Friday.

By MICHAEL H. COTTMAN
Herald Staff Writer

Johnnie Walker Red, the scotch, is seldom used as a hospital disinfectant. Then again, the penthouse of the Cricket Club is seldom used as a maternity ward.

When Sammy Kazab, 43, real estate broker, returned to his condo Thursday night, he discovered that his baby sitter, Julieta Noemi Lopez-Flores, had given birth to twin girls.

He dialed 911. Metro-Dade paramedic John Moore found mother and babies doing well.

The paramedic said Lopez, 29, a $100-a-week live-in baby sitter and housekeeper from Guatemala, had delivered the babies herself, using the scotch to sterilize a pair of scissors for cutting the umbilical cords.

Condo owner Kazab said she had the babies in the bathroom, borrowed blankets, dressed her newborns in clothing belonging to his 6-month-old son — then cleaned up as if nothing had happened.

Said the paramedic: "She was fully clothed, resting on the couch and not complaining one bit. She walked to the stretcher. This lady is as tough as nails.

"When we drove off, the babies were crying," Moore said. "That's the sign that everything is all right."

The ambulance took her from the Cricket Club, at 1800 NE 144th St., to North Miami General Hospital. "The situation is hard to believe because it was her first birth," said Fire Rescue Lt. Steve Arnall. "That's the way they did it years ago."

Lopez said she was hired about two months ago after a friend recommended her, and that she had been here about five months. Lopez, a slim woman, said, "The truth is, I didn't know that I was pregnant. It was a big surprise." She named her girls Julieta and Noemi.

Her immigration status is uncertain. Her babies are U.S. citizens.

Lopez

Noemi and Julieta with their grandparents in the store (1993).

More about the Twins, Their Father's Family

I'm going to talk a bit more about the twins—about them and their dad. I've always been a bit proud because he hurt me, and the only thing I wanted him to know was that two girls had been born to him. Supposedly, he had a lot of money, but he was never asked for one cent for the girls. The girls were over a year old when he was killed in Guatemala.

Another thing that made me feel really, really bad was that he had told me he was single, and after he died, I found out that he was married. He was from another city in Guatemala.

One weekend my sister came and said, "Do you want to go and meet his family? Do you want us to take the girls so they can meet their grandpa or so that their grandma will meet them?"

We just knocked on the door. We didn't notify them that we were going to come. I remember that the family thought we were going to ask for the inheritance. And the grandma wasn't sure that she wanted to see us. She finally came out and, well, the only thing that we told her was, "We came so that you could have the opportunity to meet the girls and that when the girls would grow up, they will know they had a father."

Thank God, the family never rejected the girls. I used to take them every three or four months. I always took them when I was in Guatemala. The grandma would always watch them and indulge them. They resembled their family very much.

When I came to the United States, I went to say goodbye to her. They never slighted me in any way. And while I was here, my parents, every once in a while, would take the girls to visit.

Before the girls came to the United States, they went to say goodbye to their grandma, and they asked their aunts for a picture of their dad. This year, in August, they went to Guatemala on vacation, and they spent time with their aunts. They came back very happy about having the opportunity to spend more time with their dad's family.

My family, my parents have never talked badly to them about their dad. I always tell them, "Your dad was a great person. He was a very hardworking man." I always try to find the way to tell them, because what affected me was one thing and, no matter what, he's their dad.

When the twins were here and were finishing junior high, one of them had her dad very much in mind. She had very good grades in school, and she put something in her diary about her dad. She said that the first prize that she receives here in the United States is going to be dedicated to him. And she put his name in big letters and drew hearts there in her diary.

I think that all that came because the family never instilled negative things in the girls' minds. I think that if good things are instilled in kids, they're going to grow up with a positive mind, and if people are positive, they will succeed anywhere they are. Right?

Her Husband

Let me see, I had been in this country for about six, seven months in 1992 when I met him—just by chance. My older sister had always come to do business here in Los Angeles. She would come, and we would always get together in downtown Los Angeles; I would go on one of those vans that are in front of Disneyland. I was in the van on my way to Los Angeles when the one that's my husband now was there with some friends. He heard me say I was from Guatemala and, well, he paid a lot of attention to me, telling me stories, jokes. And that's how that day I kind of told him where I lived.

Abel, Vivian, Mimi, and Abelito in their Orange County living room.

One weekend he went knocking on doors until he found where I lived. He pursued me for almost a year, until we got together. We've been together for more than seven years, and we already have a girl that's six years old. God gave us a little boy, Abelito; he's almost twenty-two months old. We've always had happiness, sadness, anger—because there are always those little things between couples. But thank God, here we are, together. And now, well, what we have to do is teach our kids good things and make it possible for them to get a good education. Up until now, we're fine, thank God.

Her Religion

I remember that my mother always taught us about God. And my mom told me that my great-grandfather was the first person that started to talk about God's word, Christian Evangelical, in the entire eastern part of Guatemala. My mom is already seventy-two, and I think she must have been a little girl when he came to talk about God's word. He suffered like Jesus Christ did. My mother told me that when he talked to people about God, people would slap him and spit on him.

My mom believes that she's now Christian because grandpa planted that seed that germinated so the family could get to know the word of God—because my grandmother, her mother, was Catholic. My mom didn't grow up Christian. She married at the age of eighteen,

At Sunday services at the Foursquare Church near her Riverside County home.

With Abelito in her Riverside County living room.

and she was nineteen when a friend invited her to visit the church in our town. And they went with my dad. My mom went to the Evangelical church that night, and she says that she passed to the front and accepted God, and ever since that day she has never stopped looking for God and going to church. Ever since we were inside her, she has always inculcated God's word.

My dad never objected to the idea that his children also learn about God. Although he didn't go himself, he always supported my mom. She used to take us to church so that we would learn about God. If we got sleepy, we would lie down underneath the pews. We grew up there.

My dad baptized us as Catholics. He wanted to have compadres. My mom would tell him, "If you want to baptize them, go ahead, but I'm not going to participate." So my dad would look for his compadres. I have my godparents in Guatemala. After they baptized me, I never saw them again. We were almost all baptized by my father.

My twin daughters have never separated from God's things. They came here when they were thirteen, and they didn't like it here—living with their stepfather. They had to go to Boston; there they are with my brother, and at the age of fourteen they got baptized because Christian baptism is different from Catholic baptism. In Christian baptism one is submerged in water; I remember that Catholic baptism is different. One is baptized as a child.

Vivian, behind Abelito, and their cousins waiting for the cake to be cut.

On a Saturday afternoon in May 2002 about thirty people came to a party for Vivian's seventh birthday at the Riverside County house. It was an introduction to their new home for many adult relatives and friends and a birthday party for the children, who waited until after the meal for the cake and the piñata.

Paco's son, Francisco, takes a final swing at the piñata.

At Vivian's birthday party, Abel and his brother, Paco, grilled steak, and most people ate in a covered open area at the side of the house. The piñata was hung from a tree on the lawn on the other side of the house.

Paco is a trucker and liked the house because it has parking for his truck tractor when he is home for the weekend. Parking was a great problem and fines an irritating expense in Orange County.

Dancing and Religion

Like I said before, sometimes with the desire that one has to see what life is like outside of Christianity, one wants to go dancing. I liked dancing a lot ever since I was a little girl. I really liked to listen to music. I would dance at home. I danced when I was fifteen until I was twenty-seven. After I had my twins, I became completely dedicated to being with them, to taking care of them, and I dropped all the outside things.

But last year I went dancing with my husband. The company where he worked then had a Christmas party at the Hyatt hotel. It was a very elegant dinner. After one drink he felt like dancing. "Let's go dance! Let's dance," he said. There was nice music, and we danced to satisfy his desire.

But in this past year, our life has changed. Because now I've felt the desire to look more for God—to look more for God and to inculcate good things in my little ones, because I think what our parents inculcated in us has helped us a lot in being very good people, because they inculcated a fear of God. Because it's even in the Bible—I can't remember the exact words, but the first commandment is, "You will love God with all your heart, with all your mind." The first commandment says that "God is the most important thing in any human being." Right? For me, it's a great blessing on God's part, having the parents that I have, because they inculcated very good principles, very good morals, and more than anything a fear of God.

The Twins' Fifteenth Birthday—Quinceañera

And another story that I have to tell—the story of their quinceañera [their fifteenth birthday ceremony]. It was last year [2000], in November. They live with my younger brother in Boston, and he gave them their little party.

My daughters wanted me to be there with them that day. They would tell me, "Mommy, it's that you are the principal one that should be here for our party because it's your party too. You're the one that is going to be fifteen, fifteen years of being a mom."

The economic situation was a bit difficult here with us, because only my husband works, and the baby was very little. Well, the girls also worked. They went with my brother to work part-time cleaning his office, and my brother gave them their money every week.

My daughters and my mom, who was in Boston, together they bought me the ticket. And since my other girl [Vivian] already had to pay for a ticket, my other two brothers and a cousin, well, they got enough money to buy the ticket for her. The baby didn't pay yet.

My older brother, who's in Guatemala: God has blessed him very much. He worked in the capital in the Supreme Court of Justice for thirteen years. My mom has always told me that there are only about three courses that he needed to take to finish his law degree, and he worked

At the quinceañera party in Boston: Mimi's mother,
Mimi's brother and his wife, Julieta (left), and Noemi (2000).

for many years for an attorney and also for several years in the Ministry of Human Relations. I think he retired from the government about a year ago. Now he has a job in a private company. Thank God, he helped me too. He sent me a few dollars so that I could go and be with my daughters for a couple of days. I was very happy.

My sister bought them their quinceañera rings. She sent them by mail, and my brothers placed the rings on them. It was a very pretty ceremony, very pretty, a Christian ceremony.

And, thank God, I had the opportunity of being with them and seeing how they live, how they are. My brother rents a three-bedroom apartment. His two little boys have their bedroom. And my girls have their bedroom. My brother has a sound system for them in their room. He gave them a TV set; he gave them a small and very nice refrigerator, their curtains on their windows, and their desk so that they can do their homework with their lamps.

My mom is very content in Guatemala with knowing that, well, the girls are fine.

A Final Wish

Mimi feels that she has missed the opportunity to study English in school and wishes that her husband would also want to study. She sees her own brother and his wife as a good example.

My sister-in-law in Boston—the one that my daughters live with—she didn't get much education in Guatemala. She came from a humble family. But she came from Guatemala very young—when she was sixteen. She says she came to work as a live-in. As soon as she could, she started going to school. She speaks the language well. And she's really intelligent. Now she's a citizen, and they send her papers asking if she wants to study.

She tells my brother that she wants to study because she's not going to be working in houses forever. In Boston work is different; she works by the hour. She works in the house, and she takes the children to school and picks them up. She does the chores around the house for the lady, and they have a car for her. So, now my brother told her that if she wants to finish high school, he will support her.

Acknowledgments

In spring 2000 I taught a new documentary photography course at the University of California, Irvine, and decided to do a photo-essay project like the one I assigned to the students. Ignoring the advice I gave them, I planned a project that involved many busy people and many sites: housecleaners, at work and in their homes. With generous cooperation from Mimi Lopez, Esperanza Mejia, Leidi Mejia, Tina Parker, and Sharon Risley, among others, I finished it by the class deadline.

By summer 2001 I knew that I wanted to do an expanded project on housecleaners—one that included life histories. I met with Esperanza Mejia; she thought the idea could work, and Mimi Lopez, Leidi Mejia, Tina Parker, and Sharon Risley agreed to participate. Esperanza had cleaned my family's house every other week for many years before taking the Monday through Friday job she now has. Mimi followed her for four years that ended as she anticipated the birth of her son in late 1999. Esperanza introduced me to Mimi (her sister-in-law) and Leidi (her sister). Friends whose houses they had cleaned for many years introduced me to Tina and Sharon. Victoria Rua and Sara Velazquez had worked for many years for another

family friend who vouched for me. All seven contacts depended on long-established relations of trust, and I hope that this book strengthens those relations.

Each participant recorded her life history for roughly an hour during a single interview session. Of course individuals varied in how long they talked and in the way they told stories. Before taping began, I asked each participant to tell about her life and how she got to her present situation and to talk some about her work and other things—whatever she considered important. I made it clear that she would have a chance to see the edited story and make changes. Each women spoke in her native language. Some dictated a measured, complete story; others made a quick overview statement and then concentrated on a few important topics. Esperanza Mejia did a second short interview, and Victoria Rua, at her request, taped for another forty minutes while alone a few weeks after the interview session. Later I clarified some details in conversations with participants. Most of the interviewing was done in summer and fall of 2001. A few details from 2002 were added to some of the stories.

I edited the transcripts and translated most of the Spanish interviews into English. I tried to preserve both the substantive emphases and the style of each participant while making the stories shorter and clearer. Each participant reviewed her edited story to ensure that it conformed to her intentions. Some participants made changes before approving the text.

The photos and captions record the various places I photographed the participants and their families, guests, and activities.

The participants in this project are listed as co-authors on the title page to emphasize their central roles in creating the text of their life stories. I owe them many thanks for their help and also want to thank them for the cooperation and friendship that made my work with them a personal pleasure.

Among many others who helped me complete this project, I especially want to thank Carole Browner and the late Art Rubel, Michael Gonzales, Luise and Patrick Healey, Carole Uhlaner, Graciela Villatoro, and Vivian Wayne for help making contacts with participants; Philip Cohen for the demographic estimates on domestic workers in Southern California in the introduction; Pamela Kelly for legal advice; Mike Miller and Dwayne Pack for improving my computer skills over many years; and Michelle Yee for the photos of Esperanza Mejia's wedding to Brad Guerre. Deborah Penley and Edith Valencia did excellent work transcribing the interviews. Evelyn Almodovar helped in many ways, especially with her back translations of three edited English texts to Spanish—so that they could be reviewed by the participants not comfortable with English. I am indebted to Howard S. Becker and Diane Hagaman, Ellen Butler, Pierrette Hondagneu-Sotelo, Michelle Madsen-Camacho, Alice Saltzman, Erika Sanchez-Killian, David Sapir, Judy Stepan-Norris, Vivian Wayne, and Telke Woldekael and his students at the University of Redlands, who looked at/read parts or all of the various drafts. Their comments were always appreciated, and their advice was often followed. Maria Cancian helped with readings of early edited texts and a complete draft, Steven Cancian with many ideas about photos and layouts, Hanne Rasmussen with a critical idea, and Francesca Cancian in so many ways that it is impossible to list them here.